Cassino

Dominick Graham

Cassino

Editor-in-Chief: Barrie Pitt
Editor: David Mason
Art Director: Sarah Kingham
Picture Editor: Robert Hunt
Designer: David Allen
Cover: Denis Piper
Special Drawings: John Batchelor
Photographic Research: Jasmine Spencer
Cartographer: Richard Natkiel

Photographs for this book were especially selected from the following Archives: from left to right pages 4–5 Alexander Bernfes; 8–9 Imperial War Museum; 10 Bundesarchiv; 11 Ullstein; 12 Alfredo Zennaro; 13 Ullstein; 16 US Army; 17 IWM; 17 Keystone; 18–19 IWM; 21 Bundesarchiv; 22 IWM; 22–3 US Army; 24 IWM; 25 US Army; 28 IWM; 29 Ullstein; 30 Keystone; 30 US Army; 30 Ullstein; 31 US Army; 38 Ullstein; 40–1 Keystone; 42 US National Archives; 42 Keystone; 42 US National Archives; 42 Keystone; 42 Bundesarchiv; 42 Bundesarhiv; 44–5 Keystone; 45 Zennaro; 46–9 Bundesarchiv; 50–1 Keystone; 52–5 Ullstein; 56 IWM; 57 Bundesarchiv; 60 US Army; 61 IWM; 62–3 US Army; 66–9 Keystone; 70 Bundesarchiv; 94–5 US Army; 96 Keystone; 96 US Army; 102–3 US Army; 104–116 IWM; 117 Bundesarchiv; 118–9 IWM; 120 IWM/Camera Press; 71 IWM; 72 Bundesarchiv; 74–5 US Army; 76 IWM; 77 Ullstein; 84–5 Zennaro; 86 IWM; 87 Keystone; 88–91 Zennaro; 92 Keystone; 94 US Army; 121 IWM/Camera Press; 122–3 Zennaro; 134–7 IWM/Camera Press; 140–1 Alexander Bernfes; 142–3 IWM/Camera Press; 144–5 Bundesarchiv; 148–9 IWM; 150 Keystone; 150 IWM; 153 Alexander Bernfes; 154–9 Bundesarchiv; Front cover: IWM; Back cover: IWM

First Printing: August 1971
Printed in United States of America

Ballantine Books Inc.
101 Fifth Avenue New York NY 10003

An Intext Publisher

Contents

The Pyrrhic Victory

Introduction by Barrie Pitt

It cannot by any stretch of the imagination be claimed that the strategy followed by the Anglo-American armies in the Italian theatre was inspired. An advance up the long leg of Italy – a country which lends itself to defence by providing a series of natural barriers which, with a little adaptation can be made into immensely strong defensive lines – would seem to be a way of prolonging rather than shortening the war. But this is exactly what the Allies chose to do.

With the Royal Navy once again in virtual control of the Mediterranean, a greater use might have been made of seaborne landings to turn the flanks of the coast-to-coast fortifications which could only otherwise be breached by the kind of assault which had cost the French and British – and indeed the Germans – so dear during the 1914-18 war. Excuses of various kinds have been made since 1945 to explain away this apparent lack of initiative on the part of the Allied commanders – lack of landing-craft because of the priorities given to the forthcoming Operations Overlord and Anvil; the claim that amphibious landings should not be attempted outside the range of fighter cover; it has even been suggested that a war of attrition would keep large numbers of German troops tied down in Italy thus making the task of the armies fighting on the Russian and other European fronts easier.

In the event, only two such landings were made, one at Salerno and the second at Anzio. The landing at Anzio was made on the night of the 21st/22nd January 1944 by the US 6th Corps commanded by Major-General Lucas, and it was to provide 6th Corps with a clear and unopposed landing that the first phase of the Battle of Cassino was fought.

The town of Cassino with Monte Cassino to the west of it, stands near the River Rapido and athwart Highway 6 which heads north-west towards Rome. It has been said that if the Liri valley was the gateway to Rome for the armies pushing up the west side of Italy, then Monte Maio was one of its gateposts and Monte Cassino the other. Both were strongpoints in the line of defences which Kesselring had built from the Adriatic to the Tyrrhenian Sea so for the Allies to enter the Liri valley, one of these citadels must be reduced. Monte Cassino was crowned by a huge monastery of the Benedictine order which had stood on the site for four hundred years but was to be reduced to rubble by heavy bombardment before it was finally taken by General Anders's Poles. The bitter fighting which marked the opening phase of the battle in January was to continue for five months, ebbing and flowing around the town and monastery until the Polish flag with the Union Jack beside it fluttered in the mountain breeze over the heap of rubble which had once been a noble building.

Dominick Graham follows the fortunes of the units which fought at Cassino, both German and Allied, and details the actions in which they were involved. The same ground was fought over time and time again and every identifiable feature acquired a name or a distinguishing number, temporily assuming importance as the battle surged to and fro.

On the Allied side, men from many nations fought and died on the bare rocky slopes or in the shell-shattered ruins of Cassino town. There were national units from America, Britain, New Zealand, India, Nepal, the French North African colonies of Algeria and Morocco, and Poland. Of these varied nationalities, only the French colonial troops and the little Gurkhas had experience of, or had been trained in, the art of mountain warfare; the others had to learn amongst the rainswept rocks of the wintry Italian mountains where they crouched in breast-high 'sangars' – for the ground was too stony for the digging of foxholes – and the mortar and grenade reigned supreme. The problem of supplying the forward troops with food and ammunition which must all be carried by men or mules over many miles of difficult terrain, the problem of commanders keeping in touch with the positions of their units in the confused fighting, these, and many other difficulties had to be resolved in the midst of a battle against a well-trained, courageous, and well emplaced enemy.

In the conduct of the war in Italy generally, the Allied commanders do not compare favourably with their German counterparts. Against the agonisingly slow creep of the Anglo-American armies up the Italian peninsula, the skilful generalship of Marshal Kesselring stands in bright contrast; the same is true of the battles for Cassino which could be regarded as a microcosm of the campaign at large.

A controversy has raged ever since the ending of the battle as to whether the Allies were justified in levelling the monastery of Monte Cassino to the ground. German sources have consistently claimed that their troops were not within four hundred yards of the building at the time of the first aerial bombardment, but subsequently moved in to occupy and fortify the ruins. Perhaps the rights and wrongs of the matter would not have been debated so fiercly if the air attack had been swifty followed up by a ground assault and the monastery had fallen; it is the sheer longevity of the battle which has helped give it such a prominent position in the history books. So too, did the return to the military philosophy of Passchendaele Ridge where hundreds of tons of metal were rained down on a comparatively small area causing thousands of craters from which the defenders shot down the attacking infantry, and churning the land into a quagmire in which wounded men sank and were drowned.

In 1944 the heavy artillery was supplemented by aircraft which laid a carpet of bombs over the target producing an intricate chaos of rubble effectively blocking the Allied armour but giving shelter to defenders from which, as in Flanders twenty-six years before, they shot down the advancing infantry. There is an even earlier military precedent than Passchendaele, for it can be said that the victory won at Cassino was a truly Pyrrhic one.

Battle of the nations: why Cassino?

Above: **The bleak terrain around Montecassino.** ***Right, top and bottom:*** **The interior of the monastery**

Today, the Autostrada del Sole that runs from Naples to Rome passes through a gap between the grim mountains of the old Bernhard Line. Monastery Hill, scene of fierce fighting in the winter of 1943, is hardly noticeable to a driver crossing the Rapido near the village of Sant' Angelo in Teodice; the river is small and the village is like so many others.

The barren, rolling country before Cassino seems to be suitable for tanks and the Liri valley to be broad enough to allow them a passage round the town. Why, then, was it necessary to fight so bitterly for Montecassino and the town at its foot which can hardly be seen from the autostrada?

The answer is that the battles for Cassino were fought in winter when tanks could not often reach firing positions off the roads. There was no autostrada in 1944 and the slogan about 'Sunny Italy' was a bad joke. In the valley it seemed always to be raining and the commonest sight was a truck over its axles in mud. In the mountains men fought in cloud, in sleet showers, and under frosty stars. There were no roads up there at all – only mule tracks and the paths worn by the hooves of thin cattle, driven, in better times, up to the high ridges from hill farms. National Route 6, which is called the Via Casilina, is the direct, all-weather route from Naples to Rome, and passes through the town under the Monastery. In winter conditions the road-bound army had to secure it. Attempts to by-pass the town by crossing the river Rapido-Garigliano between Cassino and the sea failed to reach the Liri valley until May 1944.

A supplementary and more difficult question is why the Allies fought so obstinately through the worst of the winter weather instead of waiting

Above and below: **American troops saw little of 'sunny Italy' around Cassino. In the valley it always seemed to be raining, and in the mountains it was frosty.** ***Right:*** **A quiet cigarette after digging-in in the mud**

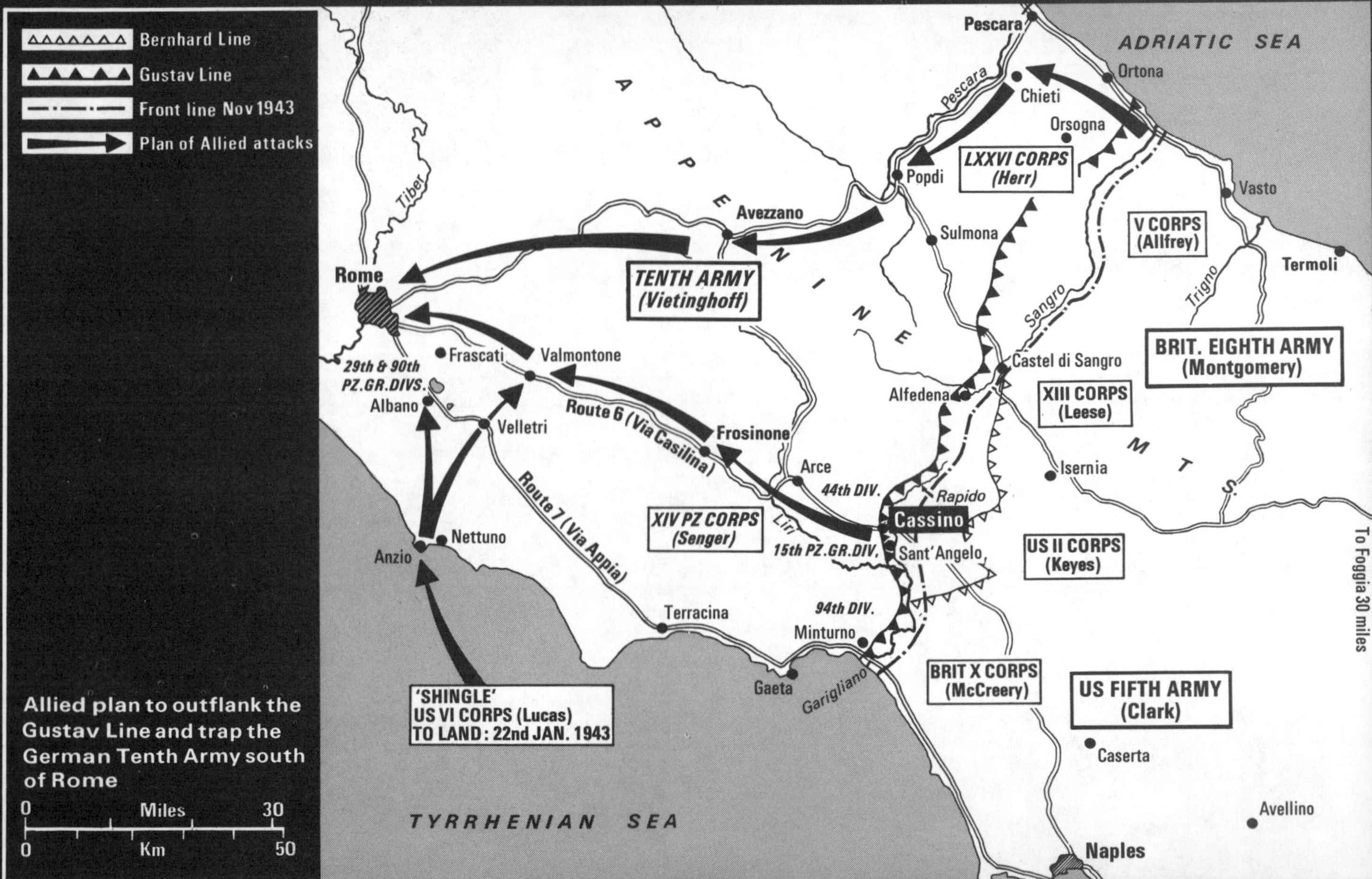

Allied plan to outflank the Gustav Line and trap the German Tenth Army south of Rome

until the mountains became more accessible and the river valleys had dried out. An answer lies somewhere in a matrix of political, military and human factors which seemed to make the bitter, winter struggle necessary and determined the course of it. This book is concerned with those factors.

The winter battles at Cassino were linked, for better or worse, with the struggle in the Anzio beachhead. The original Allied decision to land near Rome had been made on 8th November 1943, but the relation that the new operation was to bear to the main front was not decided then.

Originally, only a small force was to land to dislocate the German rear. The main drive was to come from General Mark Clark's Fifth Army which would have reached Frosinone by then, would make contact with the beachhead in seven days, and go on to capture Rome. But its slow, slogging advance through the Bernhard Line defences, and the approaching departure to Britain of most of the Italian theatre's landing craft, changed the concept. On 10th December, knowing that many of the craft could only be retained until 5th January, Clark proposed that the scope of the operation be enlarged. He believed that a stronger concentration on the German rear might panic the German Tenth Army into a retreat from the Gustav Line; Anzio might be the means of making Fifth Army's opponent relax his grip. But on the 18th, when Clark was told that he must make a final decision, the slow progress of his army forced him to recommend that the operation, code name SHINGLE, should be cancelled.

Two factors, however, conspired to change this decision.

On 8th January, General (Jumbo) Maitland Wilson was due to relieve General Eisenhower as supreme commander in the Mediterranean to allow Eisenhower to return to Britain to command operation OVERLORD. The British chiefs of staff would be primarily responsible for operations in Italy thereafter. Eisenhower and his Chief of Staff, General Walter Bedell Smith, were not anxious to pour cold water on an operation of which they had once approved, particularly if it was likely to bring about the fall of Rome before the summer. But they were not going to allow OVERLORD to be prejudiced either; and OVERLORD had priority over every other operation. In particular they insisted that the landing on the French Riviera, operation ANVIL, must not be affected. As a result, Eisenhower stood on the sidelines while SHINGLE was disinterred in late December 1943. Wilson also remained neutral, unwilling to interfere before he had assumed his new post. With both Alexander and Clark enthusiastic for SHINGLE if the conditions for its success could be provided, the way was prepared for Churchill's intervention on its behalf.

On 11th December, returning from conferences at Cairo and Teheran by way of the headquarters of the senior officers in the Mediterranean, Churchill contracted pneumonia. Eight days later he had sufficiently recovered to begin dispatching telegrams. The stagnation of the whole campaign on the Italian Front was 'becoming scandalous', he informed the British Chiefs of Staff. No use had been made of the landing craft available in the theatre since Salerno. Obligingly, the British chiefs agreed that use ought to be made of the existing craft. With this neutral admission in his pocket Churchill took the game a stage further and decided that Rome must not be sacrificed today for the Riviera tomorrow. He had never liked ANVIL because the forces for it were to be provided at the expense of the Italian theatre.

After discussions with senior officers at Tunis, it was agreed that SHINGLE ought to be undertaken with two divisions. Churchill cabled President Roosevelt to ask him to agree to the retention of the LSTs in the Mediterranean until 5th February to make this possible. Three days

General Lucas (US VI Corps) and Evelegh (British 6th Armoured Division) talk over the Anzio beachhead plans of Operation SHINGLE

later, when Churchill was at Marakesh, he heard that Roosevelt had agreed, subject to certain conditions. The meat of these was that OVERLORD and ANVIL must not be prejudiced.

Clark was delighted with the decision but his staff convinced him that unless more landing-craft were provided, some of which must be retained after 5th February, even two divisions might not survive at Anzio. So he told Alexander that while he was prepared to attack in the Liri valley with the object of drawing the maximum number of enemy reserves to that front and holding them there, (which was the only way, in his opinion, that the SHINGLE force could exercise a decisive influence on the capture of Rome) the operation was only feasible with the extra landing-craft.

Under pressure from Clark, Alexander cabled Churchill for more LSTs to strengthen the two landing divisions with tanks and artillery and for resupply; he made it clear that SHINGLE could not be undertaken without them. At a conference at Marakesh on 7th January 1944, Clark's representative insisted on the extra craft. The following day, another telegram to Roosevelt again bore fruit. SHINGLE was on: VI Corps, under General Lucas, was given the assignment.

Instead of being supplementary to and conditional on the advance of the main forces of Fifth Army, SHINGLE was now regarded as a major project. Originally, it was to take place when Fifth Army had reached Frosinone. But Clark's divisions had still not reached the Gustav Line covering the Rapido-Garigliano on 8th January. Now they had to push forward to the river line and surge across it before SHINGLE could be launched. At the very least they had to attract to themselves some of the reserve units which might otherwise face the Anzio divisions when they landed on the 22nd.

The political implications of the SHINGLE decision were important to Churchill. The Italian theatre was the only one in which Commonwealth and British forces would predominate after

General Mark Clark, firm supporter of the planned Anzio landings

General 'Jumbo' Maitland Wilson, Supreme Commander, Mediterranean

the American build-up in France. It was the only one in which he could have the main say in turning military force into political advantage. Rome might fall to Clark's Fifth Army. Clark was commander-designate of the ANVIL forces. He had asked to be relieved of that command when the SHINGLE decision was taken. This indicated that he, too, considered the battle for Rome and the possibilities opening from its capture more important.

Churchill was convinced that SHINGLE followed the classical principles of war. Allied seapower was to be used to engage more German divisions and the operation would fulfil the general object of the Italian campaign to draw more German divisions into the peninsula; at most it might lead to a decisive victory.

But there is a great gulf between the conception of a military operation and its execution. Churchill, Alexander and Clark had committed themselves to the concept of SHINGLE, but its success obviously depended on the soldiers who had to fight. To give the soldiers the best chance, the plan had to have a clear purpose; unfortunately it did not.

Fifth Army's operations on the Rapido-Garigliano were designed first to draw German reserves away from the Rome area and then to break through the Gustav Line and to link up with VI Corps. They proved to be so dispersed in space and time that the Germans were able first to stabilise the front and then to transfer troops back to Anzio, where General Lucas' VI Corps was besieged. Lucas, confused about his purpose, had missed the opportunity to disrupt the German rear areas which existed in his first thirty-six hours ashore.

In the end, SHINGLE achieved its secondary object – to engage and destroy German reserves. For while Fifth Army was attacking at Cassino through the worst of the winter weather, in order to relieve the pressure on VI Corps, the Germans were being slaughtered in the mud of Anzio by VI Corps' artillery. They, too, were trying to achieve a political victory.

Setting the scene

Field-Marshal Albert Kesselring, the C-in-C South, and his subordinate commanders, Heinrich von Vietinghoff commanding the Tenth Army and Fridolin von Senger und Etterlin commanding XIV Panzer Corps, were convinced that the Allies would attack the Gustav Line where it guarded the entrance to the Liri valley. But Kesselring was also apprehensive of landings in his rear and in mid-January, 1944, the 29th and 90th Panzer Grenadier Divisions were resting south of Rome and the 4th Parachute Division forming near the capital as a reserve available in that event. Given time, various other formations from northern Italy, France, Yugoslavia, and even from beyond the Brenner might be moved to seal off a new landing. But the 29th and 90th were his only battle-hardened, mobile reserves.

The weakest part of the German front was the coastal sector held by the 94th Infantry Division. Its flank was exposed to naval bombardment and landings from the sea, and ever since Salerno the Germans had had a healthy respect for the Allied navies' huge shells. The 94th had not been tested in battle and was not considered reliable, but its positions had been buttressed by 24,000 mines laid on the banks of the Garigliano and along the coast. Entrenched behind these and a formidable river obstacle, Senger believed that it was relatively secure. However, German Intelligence was denied the assistance of frequent aerial reconnaissance or even reliable reports from behind the lines, and it did not give the commanders adequate warning of Allied intentions. Vietinghoff was consequently surprised when two divisions of General McCreery's British X Corps assaulted the 94th across the Garigliano on the night of 17th January. Despite the mines and a landing from the sea which went astray, the British attack soon had the Germans worried.

The 94th had been informed that German boats would be operating off the coast that night and it confused the 5th Division's 'silent' attack with their own naval activity. On X Corps' right, the 56th Division succeeded in a violent assault, using most of the initial artillery support. By the 19th, despite local counterattacks, the 5th Division had seized Minturno and was three miles beyond the Garigliano and 56th Division held a bridgehead almost two miles deep.

It was intended that X Corps should roll up the southern flank of the German defences by driving northwards towards Ausonia and the Liri valley, while its third division, the 46th, assaulted across the Garigliano at Sant' Ambrogio. That town stood on a hill overlooking the junction of the Liri with the Rapido, or Gari as it is properly but less usually called at this point, and was within sight of Cassino, eight miles beyond. Then, when X Corps had attracted the German reserves, II Corps was to use the 36th Division to cross the Rapido at Sant' Angelo five miles nearer Cassino on the following night. With the Germans engaged against these bridgeheads, VI Corps would land at Anzio on the night of 21st January. It was hoped that Tenth Army would then pull back from the Gustav Line to prevent encirclement.

Prerequisite to Fifth Army's plan were two successful crossings. Combat Command B of 1st US Armored Division, which lay behind II Corps, was the only reserve available to exploit into the Liri valley. To have chosen one promising point in the line to assault and to have cracked it wide open might have been a sounder plan. For instance, X Corps' successful crossings might have been strongly exploited either north to the Liri valley or north-west up the coast. But the requirements of SHINGLE had compelled the planners to use every road leading northward to the maximum in order to close the rivers in strength and in time. Consequently, Fifth Army had reached the Rapido-Garigliano on a broad front. There was not enough time, then, to concentrate the 46th Division behind the other divisions of X Corps. Yet, it was von Senger's opinion that a breakthrough would have been achieved against his 94th Division had that been attempted.

Lack of time in which to regroup may have been the principal factor which made Clark choose to attack on a broad front. But he was also convinced that the coastal route along the Via Appia, past Gaeta and Terracina, was not suitable as a main thrust line. He preferred the Liri valley. Hence X Corps was delegated a subsidiary, although important, role in the plan. In reaching this decision he may have placed too little confidence in the effectiveness of naval bombardment. It would also have been natural for Clark to have had more confidence in his own II Corps than in the British divisions which he considered over-cautious. Finally, those Delphic Oracles, the Intelligence Staff, assured him that his enemy was tired and about to crumble and he considered this justification enough for treating the Gustav defenders as rearguards to be attacked on a broad front.

Nevertheless, SHINGLE had forced the commanders to adopt a plan which they would not otherwise have chosen. But with a little wishful thinking, they went on to make a virtue of necessity. For even a bad plan may succeed if pursued vigorously enough. Unfortunately, after X Corps' success, the vigour was mainly displayed by the Germans.

On 15th January, Kesselring's Chief of Staff, General Siegfried Westphal, had informed the Tenth and Fourteenth Armies, on the assurance of Admiral Canaris, that there was not the slightest sign that a new landing was being planned by the Allies. Only three days later X Corps' bridgehead looked as though it might expand into a breakthrough and that the fate of Tenth Army in the Gustav Line was hanging by a thread. Kesselring had to decide quickly whether to commit his reserves to support the 94th. Although

Top: **Field-Marshal Albert Kesselring, German C-in-C South.** ***Above:*** **Heinrich von Vietinghoff, German Tenth Army**

Crossing the Garigliano ***Above:*** **Italians, fighting for the Allies, load a tank raft.** ***Right:*** **A British Bailey pontoon raft**

he was only partly reassured by Canaris, his decision to do so was shaped by the knowledge that the Tenth Army's immediate reserves, parts of the Hermann Göring division, were north of the Liri and that the 29th and 90th Panzer Grenadiers could reach the southern front more easily. Furthermore, he was convinced that McCreery's attack was only the prelude to others which would be aimed at breaking directly into the Liri valley. Tenth Army's reserves must cover that contingency.

On the 19th and 20th, the 29th Division started arriving on X Corps' front. By dusk on the 21st it had halted the British and pushed them back some distance, although it had suffered heavy casualties. Indeed the casualty figures for the fighting in the hills leading to Ausonia show that the X Corps' bridgehead continued to be a running sore to the Germans throughout the winter.

Reassured about its right flank, the 15th Panzer Grenadier Division scored a right and left against the other two Allied river assaults. The 46th Division's brigade crossing at the unpromising site of Sant' Ambrogio was thrown back on the night of 19th January. Only a handful of men remained over the river in the morning and the operation was abandoned. Its failure may have been partly due to the withdrawal of DUKWs from X Corps to replace those of VI Corps which had been lost in a rehearsal for SHINGLE in Naples Bay. But it seems more likely that the determined 15th Panzer Grenadiers, in good positions, would have exacted a higher price had the DUKWs been available.

Mark Clark was disappointed over this failure for he believed that it would lessen the chances of the 36th Division the next night at Sant' Angelo. General McCreery had the opinion that against the determined 15th Panzer Grenadiers, installed in strong defences, this division would have little chance. However, Clark believed that it was essential to assault. He fully expected heavy losses but hoped that it would at least help to hold all German formations on Fifth Army's front and even draw reserves to it. The way would then be clear for SHINGLE.

In fact, Clark had already achieved both purposes by the 20th. Martin Blumenson, in *Salerno to Cassino*, wrote that the chances were that even if Clark had been aware of this, he would still have directed II Corps to carry out the next part of the operation. Despite the heavy losses he foresaw, he still needed to get into the Liri valley to begin his drive to Frosinone and the eventual link-up with the Anzio troops who were scheduled to come ashore early on 22nd January.

8th January 1944. Minturno falls to the British 5th Division

British bully beef for the Minturno refugees, their first food in days

While Eisenhower, McCreery and Mark Clark ponder the problem of Montecassino, the US VI Corps lands at Anzio on 22nd January

The validity of Clark's reasoning depended on whether the 36th Division's assault had been well conceived and would be well carried out. But he seemed to be battering at successive points in the line in hope rather than in expectation – tactics reminiscent of the First World War. There seemed to be a conflict of aims, with Fifth Army seeking both to attract reserves to itself and to break through to link up with VI Corps.

At Anzio, General Lucas knew that there had been a bloody disaster at Sant' Angelo by the evening of 22nd January. It was now clear to him that there was to be no rapid advance towards Anzio by Fifth Army. Mark Clark, visiting him on his first day ashore, remarked on his departure for Naples, 'Don't stick your neck out, Johnny, I did at Salerno and got into trouble.' Understood in conjunction with the orders he had received to advance 'on' and not 'to' the Alban Hills, which lay across the communications of Tenth Army, Clark seemed to be counselling caution.

Cautious Lucas certainly was. He spent the first three days digging in. The vital thirty-six hours when the Germans had only scattered units to oppose him, slipped by. Kesselring, always resilient in a crisis, recognised that there was no need to retreat before a static enemy which did not even harass him with active patrols. By 25th January, when Lucas did start to move forward, the immediate danger to the Germans was over.

Lucas has often been criticised for not seizing the Alban Hills. Certainly, the original concept of the operation had been that he do so. Yet without an armoured division in the assault and an adequate force to ensure its communications it was not a practical proposition. Combat Command A of the US 1st Armored Division was not in action until 29th January and by then such an operation was out of the question. However, there was an alternative to the course he chose. In the first twenty-four hours he could have mounted an armoured reconnaissance in force using the armour in his infantry divisions. It might have prevented the chaotic collection of units and parts of units – all that the Germans had available at first – from building up a defence line. The Germans might then have had to withdraw further from the beachhead and to commit more troops to contain it.

Clark, as much as Lucas, must be held responsible for the deadlock at Anzio. When he visited Lucas on 22nd January it was clear enough that the main front needed VI Corps' help, rather than the reverse. For on the night of the 20th and through the two long days that followed, the men of the 'fighting 36th', wearing their sky-blue arrowhead patches with a T for Texas on their shoulders, had been destroyed as a division at Sant' Angelo.

The site of the crossing was inauspicious. The Germans were strongly entrenched in the ruins of the village which the Todt organisation had prepared for defence. They dominated the river, which ran close under the village in an arc, and the water meadows on the far side. The 36th Division had not patrolled on its own side of the river actively enough to permit systematic mine clearance or even to prevent the Germans from laying fresh ones. The men had not patrolled effectively at all on the German bank. The approaches to the valley bottom were severely restricted and the water meadows were exposed and boggy. The river itself was swiftly flowing and in many places had steep, muddy banks. To make matters worse, the

The Anzio beachhead *Left:* Bren carriers wait to move inland. *Below:* The first clashes were 48 hours after the landings

General Truscott, US 3rd Division

General Walker, US 36th Division

General Keyes, US II Corps

General Rodt, 15th Panzer Division

Above: 22nd January. Bringing in the wounded after an attempt on the Rapido

Below: 24th January. An 81mm in action on the Rapido front

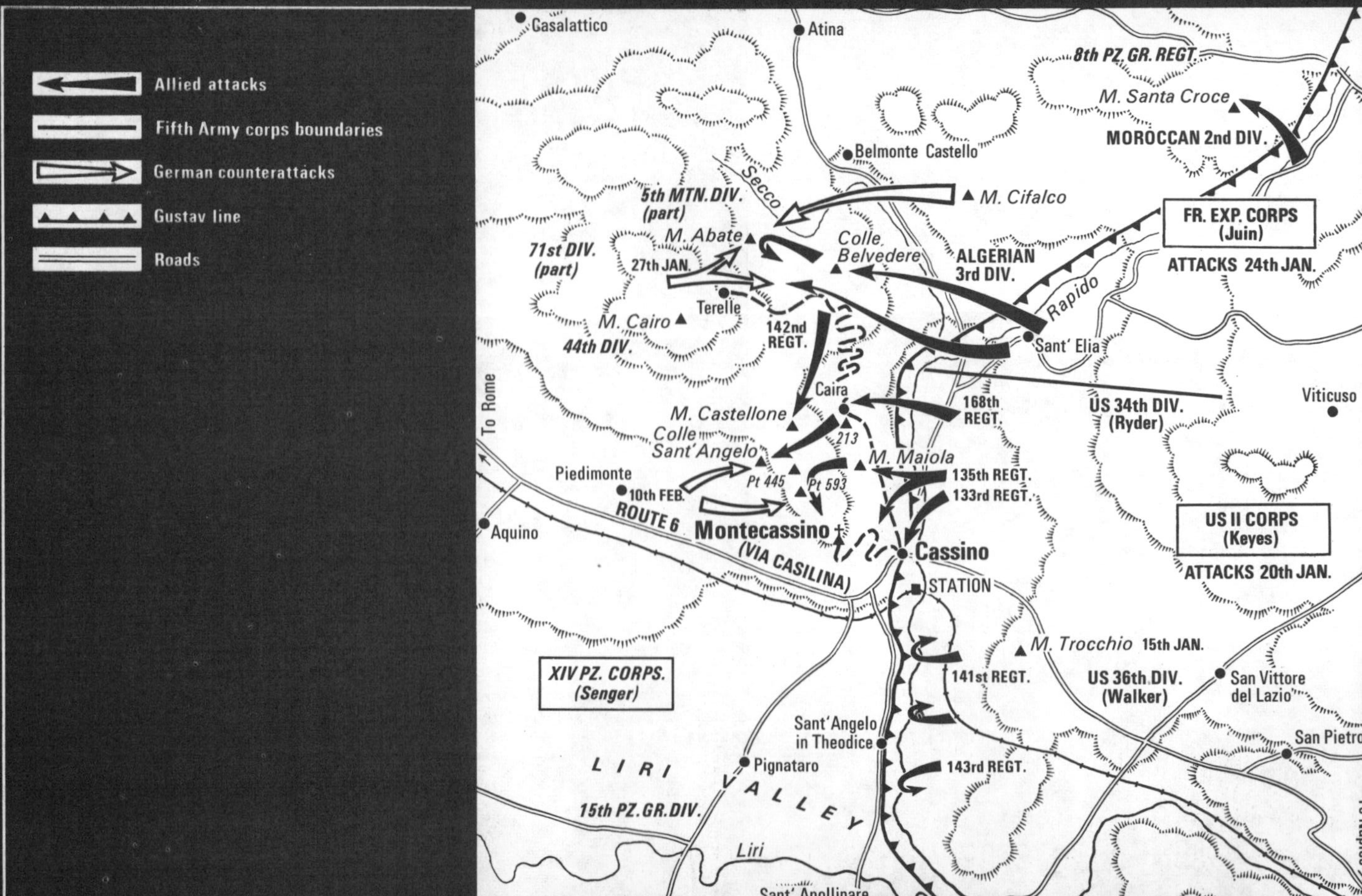

Allied attacks
Fifth Army corps boundaries
German counterattacks
Gustav line
Roads
Casalattico
Atina
8th PZ. GR. REGT.
M. Santa Croce
MOROCCAN 2nd DIV.
Belmonte Castello
Secco
M. Cifalco
FR. EXP. CORPS
(Juin)
ATTACKS 24th JAN.
5th MTN. DIV.
(part)
M. Abate
Colle Belvedere
ALGERIAN
3rd DIV.
71st DIV.
(part)
27th JAN.
Terelle
Rapido
M. Cairo
142nd
REGT.
Sant' Elia
44th DIV.
To Rome
Caira
168th
REGT.
US 34th DIV.
(Ryder)
Viticuso
M. Castellone
213
Colle
Sant'Angelo
M. Maiola
Piedimonte
Pt 445
Pt 593
135th REGT.
133rd REGT.
10th FEB.
ROUTE 6
Montecassino
(VIA CASILINA)
Cassino
US II CORPS
(Keyes)
ATTACKS 20th JAN.
Aquino
STATION
M. Trocchio
15th JAN.
XIV PZ. CORPS.
(Senger)
141st REGT.
US 36th DIV.
(Walker)
San Vittore
del Lazio
Sant'Angelo
in Theodice
San Pietro
Pignataro
143rd REGT.
LIRI
VALLEY
15th PZ. GR. DIV.
To Naples
Liri
Sant' Apollinare

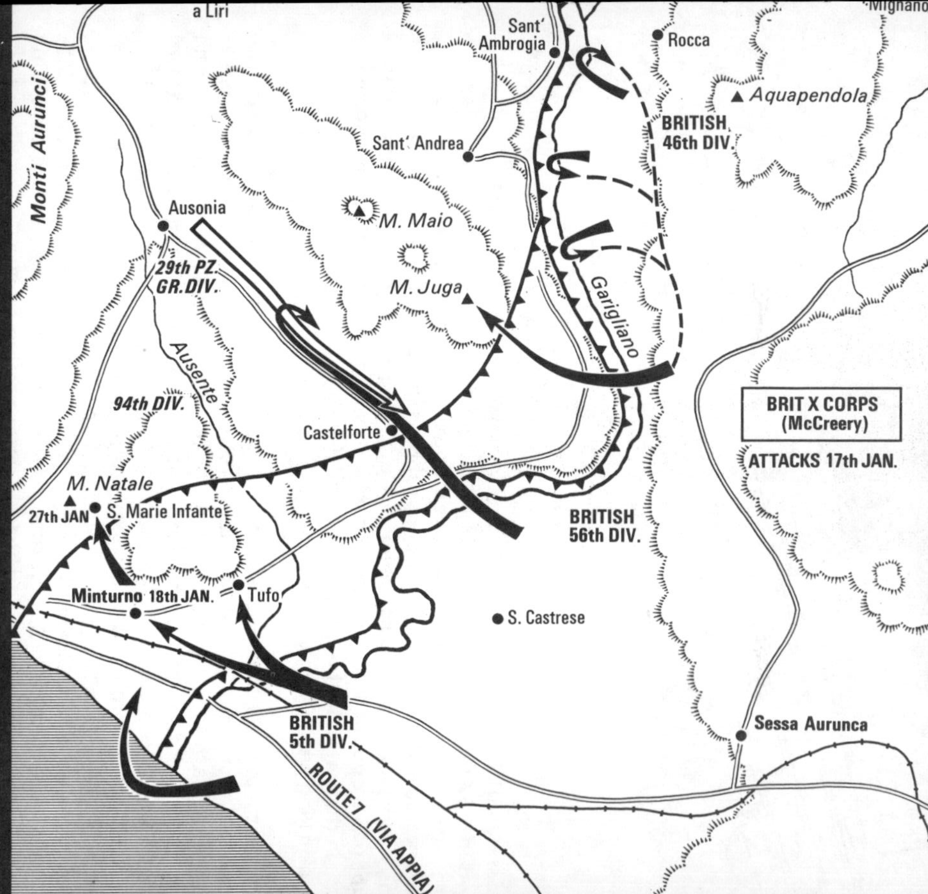

Although successful on the flanks, Fifth Army's abortive attempt to establish a bridgehead in the centre fails to breach the Gustav Line

The American DUKW amphibious transport vehicle was one of the most useful weapons in the Allies inventory, with its ability to travel with the minimum delay over ground conditions which would have stopped most other vehicles. It was of particular value in Italy for ferrying troops ashore from their trooping ships and for crossing rivers whose bridges had been blown. It weighed 14,000 pounds and could carry up to 25 troops or 5,000 pounds of cargo. It was capable of 50mph on land and 5.5 knots in the water. In the water it was driven by a propeller enclosed in a tunnel. Its range on land was 400 miles at 35mph

respective responsibilities of engineers and infantry for handling the bridging and boats were not clarified.

When the operation had first been considered in December by General Lucian Truscott, commander of the regular US 3rd Division, he had doubted whether it should be undertaken until the flanking mountains within X Corps' boundaries and those above Cassino had been cleared. At the end of the month, when it seemed that the crossing would fall to 36th Division, the commanding general, Frederick Walker, also had reservations, although he did not make strong objections. The corps commander, General Geoffrey Keyes, had proposed that II Corps should attack alongside X Corps to push into the Liri valley from the south. But General McCreery objected that his troops were not well enough equipped or trained for mountain fighting. Keyes' proposal was consequently dropped. Later McCreery admitted that Keyes' plan ought to have been followed. And as X Corps later had that role to play but without the assistance of II Corps, it might appear that Anglo-American rivalry and Clark's determination to avoid bad feeling in his own corps had something to do with his decision to use Keyes' II Corps further north.

As 36th Division's H-hour approached, Walker committed his doubts to his diary:

'We might succeed but I do not see how we can. The mission assigned is poorly timed. The crossing is dominated by heights on both sides of the valley where German artillery observers are ready . . . The mission should never have been assigned to any troops with flanks exposed. Clark sent me his best wishes . . . I think he is worried over the fact that he made an unwise decision when he gave us the job of crossing the river under such adverse tactical conditions. However, if we get some breaks we may succeed.'

Walker's fears for his flanks were exaggerated. The value of observation from Monastery Hill was nothing compared to the immediate control exercised by German observers on the battlefield. And an artillery officer would not give much for an observation post as far away as Sant' Ambrogio when smoke and mist, let alone darkness, covered the approaches to the river. The decision to attack at Sant' Angelo may have been a bad one, but it was the conduct of the battle by Walker's staff which made it a disaster. The plan was imposed on the assaulting units from above, perhaps to pre-empt their objections that the operation could not be prepared and launched within five days of their reaching the river. As General Jackson has written in *The Battle for Italy:* 'Eighth Army's ponderous build-up of guns and ammunition, its careful reconnaissance of the enemy positions, its deception plans and its rehearsals all seemed old-womanish. II Corps approached the Rapido as if it was attacking enemy rearguards . . .' Certainly X Corps had profited from British techniques in the set battle. The 36th Division had neither enough time to prepare for a difficult river crossing nor the knowledge to use the time had it been given. The habit of sneering at British caution, on this occasion, covered an opposite American vice of 'muddling through'.

After a grisly night of smashed boats, newly discovered minefields, lost units and horrible concentrations from *nebelwerfers* and heavy guns, Walker was ordered to send the battered 141st and 143rd Regiments of his division back across the river the next afternoon and night. Keyes had been pressed by Clark for results. But the Bailey bridges which alone would have allowed the tanks and tank destroyers to cross could not have been built under the blistering small arms fire even if the mud, muddle and shelling had allowed them to be brought forward. Footbridges, without handrails and slippery with mud, were soon smashed so that the toe-hold on the far bank could not be reinforced quickly even with infantry.

As the miserable second night gave way to a misty, smoky, and equally noisy morning, the defensive firing on the far bank slackened. Walking wounded accompanied by 'helpers', shock cases and even deserters, came back in large numbers. The 36th Division had shot its bolt. During the afternoon of the 22nd the operation was abandoned and the long agony ended.

The Rapido failure left a scar which was slow to heal. The division lost over a thousand men killed and missing and over 600 wounded. Most of them were in infantry battalions. The price had to be paid in broken friendships and disrupted teams. Trust and knowledge among the members of new squads had to be built again. When the division fought in the mountains behind Montecassino two weeks later, its battalions were at 30% strength and had no urge to attack.

Bitterness between Walker, Keyes and Clark was born and the profound distrust of the men in units for the staff, always easily awakened and liable to become chronic in war, took dangerous hold. Fortunately, the damage which General Rodt's division had inflicted was concealed from the Tenth Army. Rodt's report stated modestly only that they had 'prevented enemy troops from crossing Sant' Angelo'. In fact, not even his divisional reserves had been required.

The 36th Division disaster emphasized the corner into which the Allies had been led by their strategy. Clark still felt he needed to assist the Anzio landings by forming a bridgehead over the Rapido and by releasing tank forces into the Liri valley. He was now forced to seek his aims north of Cassino. Despite the unsuitability of Italian winter weather for any kind of operations, let alone armoured ones, Clark was dragged into continuing the offensive on more unpromising ground.

The struggle for the heights begins

A German mortar crew in action against a British supply column

At the post-mortem, Clark said that he shared any blame for the disaster at Sant' Angelo with the commanders on the spot. He said that he had known how difficult it would be but that some blood had had to be spilled either on the main or on the SHINGLE front and he greatly preferred that it be on the Rapido, 'where we were secure', rather than at Anzio, 'with the sea at our back'. He had now decided to attack over the high ground to the north of Cassino. 'This is what he should have done in the first place',Walker confided to his diary. But the problems there were likely to be just as serious. The defences of Cassino town were believed to be well prepared and so the aim was to outflank them by a turning movement from the north. The Liri valley might then be reached at Piedimonte San Germano or, perhaps, by means of a wider hook through Belmonte, Atina and the Melfa river valley leading to Roccasecca.

Whichever operation were chosen, formidable mountain positions would have to be assaulted. The Germans might not be so numerous in the mountains but they would enjoy greater natural advantages than they had on the Garigliano. Fifth Army operations would have to start from the Rapido valley north of Cassino. Not only would they be overlooked from the Cassino Massif to the south but also from Monte Cifalco to the north and from the huge, snow covered slopes of Monte Caira in the west. There was a good road leading up the valley from Route 6 to Belmonte but the ground on either side of it was a bog; and to mount a flank attack towards Terelle, first the bog and then the Rapido had to be crossed. Beside that, the road to Belmonte originated in Cassino town, which was still held by the Germans.

Artillery support for infantry in the mountains presented a technical problem. Crests intervened between gun and target along the normal trajectory of shells. Not only were guns unable to hit some targets but if they tried their own troops might suffer. In order to overcome this difficulty, weapons designed to do so would fire in their upper registers in order to achieve plunging fire. But this could not be done at the long ranges made necessary because field guns close to their targets would have been in full view of the Germans. Necessity forced the artillery to concentrate their guns behind the shield of Monte Trocchio or in the valleys near Portella. But even then the shortage of smokeless propellent for use in daylight and flashless propellent for use at night enabled the Germans to plot the location of Allied guns accurately.

The most effective weapon against the narrow ridges and steep reverse slopes common in the mountains was the mortar. But the range of the 3-inch or 81mm mortars in infantry battalions, or even the heavier mortars of the artillery, was quite short. The tubes had to be close up to the infantry; this in turn meant that the weapon and supplies of bombs be carried up into the mountains.

Troops required a great deal of preparation if they were to use mountainous terrain to their advantage. One of the basic material operational requirements needed by a division in the mountains was a formidable supply of mules (about 2,000) and jeeps. Clothing and footwear had to be suitable for use in extremes of temperature, snow and ice, and long periods of rain. Support weapons had to be pack-operated. Just as important was the physical and mental preparation the soldiers had to undergo if they were to give a good account of themselves. Out of ten men under the age of thirty from the streets of any Western city, not more than one or two can climb up a track at the standard rate of 1,000 feet an hour. Ask them to carry forty or fifty pounds on their backs and the failure rate will be much higher. Yet battalions had to ascend 2,000 feet above the valley floor to the summits they were to assault. Add to the discomfort of physical exertion the miseries of exposure to winter weather and the high probability of violent death, and you have the lot of the infantryman in the mountains north of Cassino.

The maintenance of discipline in the mountains was a special problem. Men had to be taught to avoid excessive sweating by shedding clothing, to change their socks in order to keep themselves clear of trench foot, to build defensive stone *sangars* and to lie hidden in them for hours on end despite the calls of nature. Isolated infantrymen who could talk only to the one or two others who shared their holes became unreliable unless they were carefully nursed by their officers and NCOs. It was not difficult for them to straggle when they felt they had

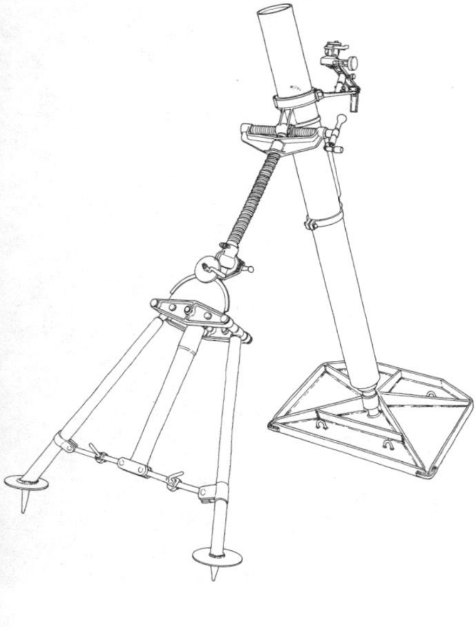

The British 3-inch mortar was the standard mortar used by battalion heavy weapon companies, and was a very accurate piece of equipment. *Weight:* 124lbs (mortar 42lbs, mounting 45lbs and base plate 37lbs). *Length:* 51 inches. *Effective range:* 1,600 yards. *Weight of bomb:* 10 lbs. *Rate of fire:* five rounds per minute

taken enough, or even when they tired on the climb up the track from civilisation at the bottom of the mountain.

Considering the conditions and the unsuitability of some of their equipment, the performance of the US 34th Infantry Division, a National Guard outfit, in coming within an ace of cracking the mountain defences of Cassino, is almost beyond praise. The brilliant, mountain-trained French North Africans on their right, showed that Cassino might have been outflanked had there been more of them and had they been better supported.

The French had opened the Fifth Army operations which were designed to draw German reserves away from Anzio to the northern and southern flanks of the Gustav Line so that II Corps could break into the Liri valley. The 2nd Moroccan Division and the newly arrived 3rd Algerians had been pressing forward towards Belmonte and Atina even before X Corps attacked. When Clark decided to exert a shorter turning movement round Cassino, the corps commander, General Alphonse Juin, was ordered to redirect his division further south onto the high spur between the Terelle and Belmonte roads. This reorganisation would take him two days which meant that the Algerians, who were to attack, would not be ready until 25th January.

A day earlier, General Charles Ryder's 34th Division on the French left would cross the Rapido and thrust southward along the river into Cassino town, while a right hook would drive into the mountains to seize Monte Castellone.

Fifth Army Headquarters began the winter battles with the impression that the enemy's strength was ebbing away due to casualties, exhaustion, and possibly falling morale. It seemed inconceivable that the 26,000 casualties that Fifth Army divisions had suffered since the crossing of the

Italian porters carry Allied supplies to the Cassino front line

General Schlemm German I Para Corps

General Juin, French X Corps

General Franck, German 44th Division

General Ryder, US 34th Division

Volturno had not been reflected in proportionate enemy losses. What then was the state of the German divisions which were defending Cassino?

The New Year had opened with blizzards in the high Appenine Mountains. The snow was breast-high in places and even patrolling was impossible for the 5th Mountain Division which faced the French. The division had come from the Russian front. Its administration was chaotic because much of its equipment was marooned in snowbound trains somewhere back up the line. Sixty per cent of its motor transport was under repair and food for its first line units was sometimes forty hours in transit. Furthermore, the division was much under-strength and was not properly trained or equipped for the rôle it had to play.

By the afternoon of 15th January, hammered by French attacks northeast of Sant' Elia, at Madonna di Raditto, the 5th Mountain Division was cracking. It was 'no longer a viable fighting unit as the French had unfortunately proved themselves to be very good fighters'. Small measures would not suffice to restore the situation, Kesselring thought. Convinced that he had nothing to fear on the Eighth Army front by the evident weakness of the 1st Canadian Division and the 8th Indian Division, he decided to thin out opposite them and reinforce XIV Panzer Corps. He therefore ordered the 3rd Panzer Grenadier Division to move south to relieve 5th Mountain. That division would then sidestep over the passes to relieve 305th Infantry who, in turn, would take over from 3rd Panzer Grenadiers.

On 5th Mountain Division's right was the 44th Infantry Division, shortly to be commanded by General Franck. Its condition had been improving and it had pulled back into the Gustav Line on a front from Portella to just south of Cassino on the night of 15th January in unhurried fashion. Its battalions averaged 250 men which, by German standards, was acceptable.

Cassino town was to be defended by part of 71st Infantry Division, but owing to heavy air attacks on 15th January, it arrived from the north in driblets – a customary practice for German formations. However, the 211th Grenadier Regiment had moved into the line just south of Cassino by 16th January. A second regiment of the division, the 191st, was beginning to arrive. The support for the 44th, the 71st and 5th Mountain Divisions was increased to twenty-four troops of field guns and *nebelwerfers;* about 50% of XIV Panzer Corps' available artillery.

Locating Allied divisions was always a difficulty for the Germans, but the state of their Intelligence had been worse than usual since Vietinghoff's Chief of Staff, Wentzell had allowed his Intelligence Officer to go on marriage leave. The capture of a prisoner from the 4th Tunisian Regiment seemed to indicate fresh French troops which would be disconcerting on XIV Corps' already shaky left wing. The US 3rd Division was unaccounted for and there was believed to be a second US armoured division on the Via Casilina which augured a narrow frontal attack on the Cassino sector.

Thus, when X Corps attacked, 94th Division was completely surprised. XIV Corps reacted by hurrying the reconnaissance battalions of 44th and 71st Infantry Divisions and the 3rd Panzer Grenadiers to form a reserve behind the threatened sector. The relief of 5th Mountain was halted and those units already relieved were held in XIV Corps reserve. Units of the Hermann Göring Division, under orders for France, were recommitted and its reconnaissance battalion was brought over from the LXXVI Corps front on the Adriatic. Parts of 1st Parachute Division were placed at short notice to follow it. Kesselring ordered all these moves, as well as those of 29th and 90th Panzer Grenadiers, before he had heard for the first time that the 5th Division from the British Eighth Army was in the X

Corps attack. It was clear to him that Fifth Army planned to strike up the Ausente valley with X Corps and then commit II Corps against 15th Panzer Grenadiers.

The 29th Panzer Grenadiers had reached Esperia before evening on 18th January. On the 19th, General Schlemm's HQ I Parachute Corps from the Rome area was ordered to take command on the 94th Division's front. Schlemm was told to commit the 29th as soon as they were ready. They attacked at 1130 hours on the 21st, despite a standing embargo against daylight attacks. Kesselring was always chastising the 29th, one of his best divisions, and he sent them a personal reprimand for being slow to organise on this occasion. Yet they halted the British attack. The 90th, owing to administrative muddles and the bombing of Sulmona railway station, was not ready to receive orders until 21st January.

The Germans might be said to have over-reacted to X Corps' offensive. Wentzell remarked that on the night of 20th January the roads from LXXVI Corps south were so laden with traffic that 'not another apple could fall to the ground'. And when a prisoner from the British 46th Division was interrogated at Sant' Ambrogio, 15th Panzer Grenadiers jumped to the conclusion that they were about to be attacked by two US armoured divisions and the US 3rd Infantry Division. The 90th Panzer Grenadiers were therefore kept in reserve until the night of 21st January when the 36th Division showed its hand at Sant' Angelo. They were then unmercifully strafed by X Corps fighter bombers and only a regiment reached the battle on the 5th Division's front. It is interesting to conjecture how much more effectively German divisions would have been tied down had the 36th Division not been committed at all.

No sooner had Schlemm and his

staff taken over the conduct of operations opposite X Corps than SHINGLE started. At 0830 hours on the morning of 22nd January, he was ordered to re-establish his headquarters south of Rome and take control of the units assembling to seal off the new beachhead. In the next few days, the flow of units from LXXVI Corps and Army Group Reserve to XIV Panzer Corps was replaced by one towards the new threat. The 3rd Panzer Grenadiers, less the units already committed opposite the French right wing, was despatched and 26th Panzer was moved to Avezzano from the Adriatic. However, the main reinforcement had to come from northern Italy, Yugoslavia and even further afield. But snow and ice, the bombing of railway junctions, and normal operational chaos prevented more than a trickle of them arriving before

Left and below: **French and German artillery. The terrain reduced the role of tanks, emphasising artillery**

25th January. Meanwhile, the breach had to be filled by elements of many formations already south of Rome. In consequence, a concise estimate of the influence on the Germans of operations on Fifth Army's main front is difficult. For instance, parts of the 29th and 90th Panzer Grenadiers were never drawn south to face X Corps and were in Schlemm's I Parachute Corps by early morning of 23rd January. Even parts of 71st Infantry, including its headquarters, and of the Hermann Göring Division were also gathered in.

On balance, the effect of Clark's operations was that XIV Panzer Corps was strengthened at the expense of LXXVI Panzer Corps and that the number of troops committed against both parts of Fifth Army was greatly increased at the expense of German reserves and occupation forces. General Traugott Herr declared that if Eighth Army attacked his weakened LXXVI Corps he would have to retreat. Senger, despite 36th Division's failure, still believed the forces opposite him were such that there was nothing to stop II Corps driving to Rome. In the evening of 22nd January he was recommending a fighting retreat into the so-called Führer and Senger switch line. He would then be able to bring into reserve the elements of 29th Panzer Grenadiers which were fighting opposite X Corps and to avoid 'the senseless destruction' of 94th Infantry and Battle Group Baade of 90th Panzer Grenadier Division. However, Kesselring not only firmly told him to stay where he was but ordered to Anzio elements of 15th Panzer Grenadiers and Regiment von Corvin of the Hermann Göring Division which was under its command.

By the end of 24th January, Kesselring considered the crisis to be over for the time being on both fronts and was planning to concentrate the 29th and 90th Divisions as a reserve under XIV Panzer Corps and to complete the concentration of 71st Infantry at

Cassino. He was even talking of pulling back the 15th Panzer Grenadiers into reserve and sending 8th Panzer Grenadier Regiment, then being battered by the French at Monte Croce, to join the rest of the 3rd Division at Anzio. This was the day on which the Fifth Army resumed its offensive, not with the large forces Senger and Vietinghoff believed were available, but with 34th US Infantry and the tiring French corps. They were faced by the 44th, parts of the 71st Infantry and elements of 5th Mountain, intermingled in the curiously disorderly fashion common to German dispositions in Italy.

The 34th had reached the Rapido opposite Cassino after bitter fighting. Its infantry had inched forward against tenacious 44th Infantry Division rearguards. When the leading companies reached the valley it was a quagmire. The Germans had diverted the river. Patrols splashed forward and found it running swiftly between steep, muddy banks or stone walls. The promising approaches to it were blocked by bands of barbed wire and overlapping leaves of mines. Immediately west of the river arose the formidable bulk of Monte Cassino. From it the Germans could observe the whole valley through the French zone and beyond it to their own positions at Monte Cifalco. Just north of Monte Cassino was a spur called Colle Maiola. From Maiola re-entrants ran down into the valley; one of them to an Italian artillery depôt at Monte Villa called 'the barracks' and the other to the village of Caira at the mouth of the valley leading up to Terelle. The valley and re-entrant from Caira seemed to offer the best route to the interior of the Cassino Massif. Somewhere up there in the clouds was Monte Castellone, one of 34th Division's objectives. Towering above everything and only visible on clear days, was the snow-covered bulk of Monte Caira, 5,500 feet high.

The barracks was the first objective of the assaulting 133rd Infantry Regiment. But the mud near the river, even more mines than had been expected, fierce small arms fire and heavy mortaring and shelling brought the attack to a halt on the near bank. In the early morning of 25th January, Ryder shifted the attack further north to avoid the fire from the barracks. Attacking with three battalions abreast and every gun that could bear pounding the barracks and the hills behind, the 133rd hacked out a shallow bridgehead. But they had not done enough to allow the 168th Infantry to pass through them and had temporarily lost the will to move forward themselves under the German fire. The battalions remained in their wet and shallow holes being hammered all through the 26th.

For the assault to succeed, it was essential to seize a bridgehead of sufficient depth that enemy anti-tank

German reinforcements move up to counter the growing Allied pressure

guns could not dominate the river crossings. If tanks could cross into the bridgehead they might be able to eliminate strongpoints by direct fire. But this had not been possible and the valley bottom was so soft that twenty tanks of the supporting 756th Tank Battalion were badly bogged on the approaches to the river and could not be recovered until the battle was over.

After a company of the 135th, the third regiment in 34th Division, had crossed on the left of the 133rd and had been pinned down before more could follow, Keyes pressed Ryder to commit more troops. He still believed that it was possible to launch armour up the Liri valley, even in the existing winter conditions, and had his eyes on Cassino town. Consequently the 168th was ordered to cross the Rapido on the right of the 133rd. With six companies of engineers working on tank tracks alone, four tanks finally got forward with the assault and were able to help the infantry carve out a shallow bridgehead by mid-day on the 27th.

Although all the tanks were knocked out by the early afternoon, and the collapse of the tracks leading to the river prevented any others from crossing, the infantry made progress alone. Their principal objectives were a grassy hill above the barracks called Point 213 and a knoll nearer Caira village, Point 56. With these captured, they might attack the barracks and then advance down the road to Cassino and in the other direction to Caira.

That night of the 27th a company reached the top of Point 213 and occupied it. And then in one of those moments of stress caused by fatigue and isolation its commander lost his nerve. He ordered his men down again. A panic started and soon two other companies retired. The regimental commander then decided to withdraw his remaining companies

Despite constant patrolling, German Intelligence was poor

which had been isolated.

The French had made progress on the right of 34th Division by this time. Attacking on 25th January, they took the Colle Grosso. By the end of the 26th they were on Belvedere above the top bend of the hairpin road to Terelle. They could not reach Monte Abate, from which they would have overlooked Terelle, until the Americans had made some progress. But from Belvedere they were able to make the German positions in Caira village uncomfortable.

Continuing the Fifth Army practice of attacking at widely spaced and unrelated places, the 142nd Infantry Regiment of 36th Division, which had not been committed at Sant' Angelo, had been ordered to assault just north of there to enable CCA of 1st US Armored Division to exploit up the Liri valley. But in order to exploit the French corps' important breach in the Gustav Line at Belvedere, Clark directed them against Caira village and Monte Castellone instead. It was the objective which 34th Division might have been given had II Corps not been mesmerized by the need to take Cassino town and burst open the door to the Liri valley. If the French and American divisions had attacked side by side some time and blood might have been saved.

With the Germans weakening, Mark Clark expected Cassino to fall quickly

With the German hold on his right loosened by the French, Ryder recommitted his 168th Infantry further north to attack across the lower ground and take Hills 213 and 56. On 29th January his tanks found a way across the river. Their appearance on the far bank proved decisive by the afternoon, although the night was far advanced before the two objectives fell. That night, the 142nd started working across the slopes behind Caira and below Belvedere in the direction of Monte Castellone. On 30th January Caira fell to a platoon of infantry and tanks of the 168th.

Ryder's next move was to commit the 135th and 142nd through the breach at Caira to exploit into the mountains between Monastery Hill and Castellone. The clouds which commonly descend from Monte Caira enveloped the advance of both regiments. The 135th occupied the Colle Maiola and the first and highest ring contour of the Castellone feature, while the 142nd reached the Massa Manna feature, only a kilometre from Terelle. Both objectives were seized on 1st February almost unopposed. Towards Cassino town the narrow passage between the Rapido and the hills was still blocked by the barracks. The 133rd attacked and cleared it after bitter fighting on 1st and 2nd February but when tanks and infantry tried to exploit towards Cassino they were halted by anti-tank and machine gun fire.

From Fifth Army headquarters the prospect now looked favourable. 'Present indications are that the Cassino heights will be captured very soon,' Clark informed Alexander. Hoping for a breakthrough, Alexander had already brought the New Zealand 2nd Division over the mountains from the Eighth Army front on 30th January. And when it was clear to him that the Gustav Line at Cassino town would not be broken, he ordered Lieutenant-General Sir Oliver Leese, Montgomery's successor, to send the 4th Indian Division to join the New Zealanders. The two divisions would form a temporary New Zealand Corps under the veteran warrior, General Sir Bernard Freyberg to finish or exploit II Corps' operation. Two brigades of the Indians were still crossing the Appenines on 3rd February when 5th New Zealand Brigade relieved the weak 141st and 143rd Regiments of 36th Division in order that they could reinforce 34th Division's effort in the mountains behind Cassino.

Ryder's divisional operations report for January contained this passage: 'Fighting was the bitterest met to

date; casualties from all causes were high; replacements were slow in arriving and were inadequate in number. Nevertheless, with 33 days of front line duty behind them, 28 of which had been spent in sanguinary conflict, the period ended with the 135th Infantry attacking thru the 168th Infantry to capture the high ridge which dominated the valley and barred further progress of the 5th Army to the northwest.'

While the 135th was resuming its attacks in the hills, the German

Fourteenth Army, formed under General Mackensen to control operations at Anzio, was beginning the first phase of its counteroffensive.

Before the SHINGLE adventure, there had been no military necessity for aggression against the Gustav Line during the winter; now that VI Corps at Anzio was not only contained but threatened, immediate and continuous aggression at Cassino seemed essential. Watching his Anzio force behaving like a stranded whale rather than a wildcat, Churchill

With every advance by Fifth Army came the problem of mine clearing

urged the commanders to keep attacking the Germans. 'We have a great need to keep continually engaging them, and even a battle of attrition is better than standing by and watching the Russians fight.'

Indeed, the struggle at Cassino in February and March was to follow a similar pattern to that set by the battles of attrition of the First World War.

Hope, fear and failure

It had been touch and go for the Germans. 26th January in particular was a day of crisis. The 132nd Grenadier Regiment of the 44th Division halted the Americans in the marshes opposite Monte Villa, but the two battalions of the 191st Grenadiers from 71st Division which lost Belvedere and the entrance to the Secco valley leading to Belmonte to the French were very hard hit. A small number of French tanks tried to break through to Belmonte but were stopped by artillery fire. XIV Corps was convinced that an armoured formation was working with the French. 2nd/191st and some engineers, held in reserve near Terelle, went forward to retake Belvedere but failed. To Schmidt von Altenstadt, the new Chief of Staff of XIV Panzer Corps, it appeared that the French would take Terelle within hours, thus 'causing the Cassino block to cave in from the north'.

Von Altenstadt combed the southern front for reserves. But X Corps was attacking again and on the 27th it forced the redoubtable 29th Panzer Grenadiers off Monte Natale and Monte Rotondo. Colle Ceracoli was also under attack in 15th Panzer Grenadiers' sector. Consequently, only two of the battalions of the third regiment of 44th Division, the 134th, could be spared to move north into corps reserve in the Belmonte area.

A German patrol moves out on the slopes of the Mountain

1st/134th went into action there on the evening of the 26th, but was halted by artillery fire. 3rd/134th reinforced two battalions of the 191st and one of the 131st which was sealing off the French salient. The 94th Division's reconnaissance battalion was sent to the Atina area from the south.

The pattern for German tactics at Cassino was already taking shape. Kesselring controlled the use of reserves because he had to balance the needs of Fourteenth Army at Anzio with those of the Tenth at Cassino. He milked divisions elsewhere, unit by unit, to reinforce these two *Schwerpunkt*. As a result the front was held by groups of units and not by divisions at all. But as the Allies employed single divisions, whose activities were not closely related to those on their flanks, which were not reinforced and which consequently grew weaker by the day, German piecemeal defence methods, although they were adopted by necessity, became a virtue.

On the 27th, 15th Panzer Grenadier Division had to extend its left boundary to cover the positions vacated by the 134th Grenadiers and von Senger still expected an attack on Cassino town from the east. Kesselring visited 44th Division and XIV Corps on that day and calmly announced that the Allies were not strong enough to break through north of Cassino. He had been encouraged in this belief when 2nd/191st chased the French off Monte Abate on which they had

The Germans were content to maintain a largely defensive role around Cassino until the Anzio beachhead had been eliminated

A damaged tank, one of the many German casualties of the heavy Allied artillery concentration. Senger was considering stopping daylight raids

gained a foothold, and 1st and 3rd/134th retook the top of the road from Caira to Terelle. Caira itself was still firmly held. It looked to both Tenth Army and Army Group headquarters that the French had been brought to a standstill, for which Vietinghoff was 'deeply thankful'.

Senger was never given to premature optimism and reminded his superiors of the casualties his units had suffered from artillery fire. In future, daylight counterattacks might have to be replaced by night raids. The worst was yet to come, he thought. And he ordered 2nd/361st Panzer Grenadiers of the 90th Division across to Arce, twenty kilometres up the Liri valley, and sent 2nd/134th, the last reserve behind 15th Panzer Grenadiers, to Monte Castellone. A field replacement-holding battalion and a company of German Air Force ground troops were hurried to the Monte Abate area. Kesselring himself could only promise that the element of the 90th, which was fighting at

Above: **German dugouts on the slopes of Hill 569.** ***Right:*** **German shelling was destroying Allied communications**

Anzio as Battle Group von Behr, might be returned to Cassino 'within the next few days'.

It was as well that Senger acted, for on the 29th the French were again attacking at Monte Abate and in the Belmonte valley and were threatening to take Terelle by an advance up the road. Senger reacted by taking 3rd/131st out of the line south of Cassino and sending it to Monte Castellone, and he extended the front of 5th Mountain, on whom the pressure had been eased, to include the Belmonte valley.

At a conference at his headquarters that day, Senger told Wentzell that he believed that the Terelle thrust was the most dangerous. Even though the Allies seemed to be employing no more than two French regiments there and a third US one was reported to be coming forward, the artillery concentrations were so heavy that he

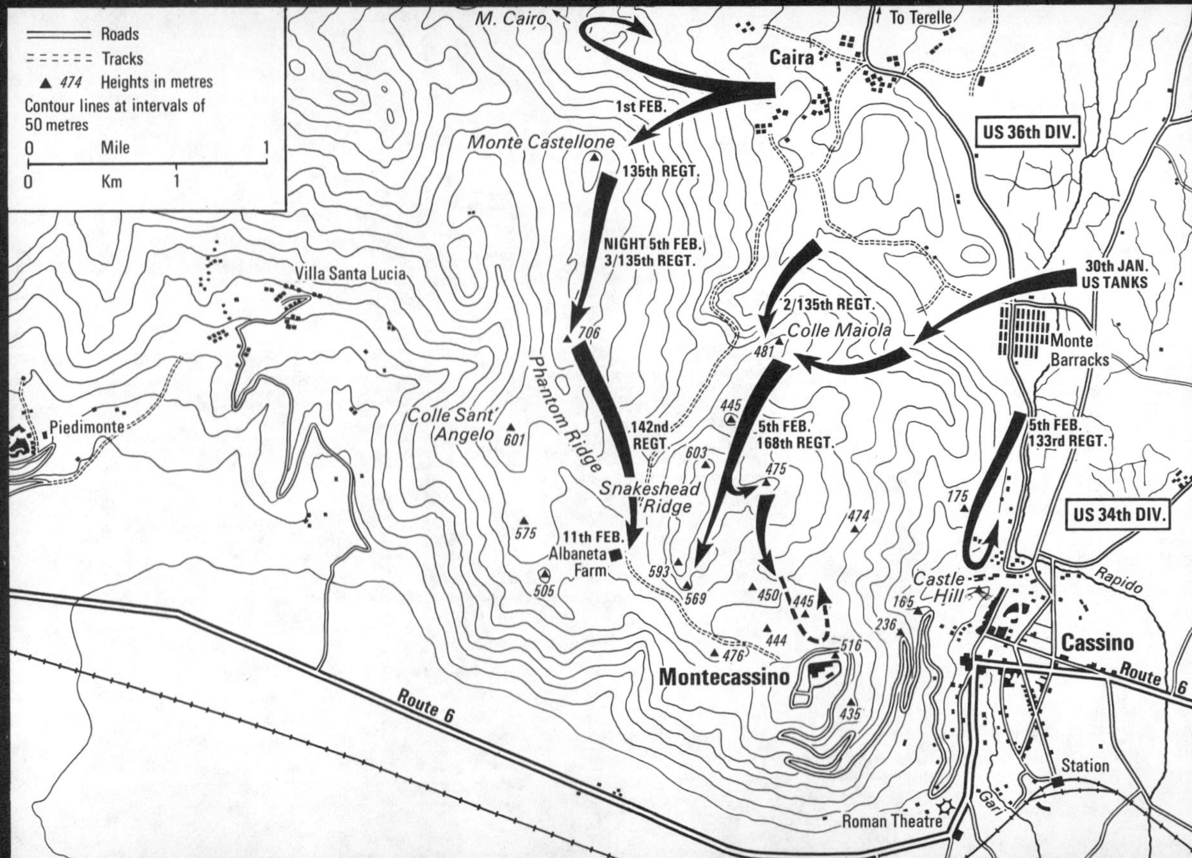

US II Corps attack on Montecassino is brought to a halt (30th January/12th February)

believed they realized the importance of it. The British in the south were systematically destroying the units of 94th Infantry and 29th Panzer Grenadiers, and although they were no longer believed to be intending an operation 'in the grand style', they were preventing him from pulling out any more units of the 90th and using them to release 211th/71st for use in the Castellone sector. Although he was losing men at the rate of a battalion a day in the north, 29th Panzer Grenadiers' casualties for the period 21st-31st January were heavier than any other formation.

Wentzell clarified a number of points about the future for Senger. The Cassino block had to be held until the Anzio bridgehead had been eliminated by Fourteenth Army. When that was done, he could expect to be reinforced and he might take the offensive. On the other hand, if Mackensen failed, a new situation would arise. Senger cited the inadequacies of the Senger-Riegel switch line through Piedimonte and declared that the Gustav Line was more economical in manpower. If a withdrawal became necessary, he thought that XIV Corps ought to go right back to the area of the Alban Hills. But Wentzell told him that no withdrawal from Cassino was contemplated at the moment. Senger would have to take risks in other sectors to find the men to hold it.

Once the Germans had made up their minds to hold the Cassino block at all costs, they thinned out their line elsewhere even more ruthlessly. On the 31st, the 3rd Battalion of the 3rd Parachute Regiment was ordered south from the Adriatic and a battalion from the 200th and another from the 361st Panzer Grenadiers arrived. Both were from the 90th Division. Their division commander, General Baade, was appointed to command the Cassino sector on the same day.

30th January had been another bad day at Caira village and along the Rapido. A large force of American tanks, having forced their way over the river the day before, shot up the bunkers of 1st/132nd Grenadiers, one by one, forcing the survivors up on to the Colle Maiola behind. Thirty-five men of the 191st, all that were left, were pushed off Monte Abate by the French that night. On their right, 2nd/134th, with only thirty men remaining, withdrew towards Terelle. The remnants of the men from Caira, together with 2nd/132nd and the newly arrived 2nd/361st Panzer Grenadiers, began to prepare a makeshift switchline between Monte Castellone and Villa Santa Lucia on the 31st. The three battalions of the 131st Grenadiers moved to cover the road to Terelle on either side of Massa Manna. But by the time they got there the US 142nd Regiment had forced the handful of defenders from the 134th back into Terelle.

The 142nd were slow to follow up and there was time for 1st/8th Panzer Grenadier Regiment of the 3rd Division to arrive at Terelle on 1st February from 5th Mountain Division's zone on the left. An Alpine battalion from LXXVI Corps also started on its way from the Adriatic. But XIV Corps was now sure that the French were exhausted and that the Americans intended to switch the main thrust southward round the back of the Monastery towards Villa Santa Lucia.

The new danger sector was between Castellone and Colle Maiola. Castellone itself was reported to have been occupied by two American companies in the mist on 1st February. A counterattack by 15th Panzer Grenadiers' engineer battalion failed to dislodge them, but two companies of 2nd/361st Panzer Grenadiers prevented the 135th Infantry from advancing over the col towards Monte Caira. The rest of the battalion blocked the Americans on Colle Maiola.

Baade at once began to reorganise the defences of Cassino when he arrived on 1st February. A flamboyant, stormy figure, he demanded fresh troops, and made them a condition for

A good view of the Monastery and, rising above it, snow-covered Mt Caira

stabilising the front. As a start, 3rd Parachute Battalion arrived to throw the Americans off Castellone, which Baade considered his main task. His own 1st/361st Panzer Grenadiers was pulled out from the X Corps front together with anti-tank, field artillery and engineer battalions from the 94th. 3rd/8th Panzer Grenadiers followed their 1st Battalion from 5th Mountain's front.

However, the activities of the 34th Division on 2nd February gave Baade no time to mount a counterattack and he found that he had to use the parachutists to plug holes in his front. Kesselring was not much concerned at the US 133rd Regiment's attack in the valley from Monte Villa towards Cassino town, but he was determined to reinforce behind the Monastery until the massif was safe. He told Baade that he was to have another parachute battalion from the Adriatic and even the division's Machine Gun Battalion from Anzio. 2nd 200th Panzer Grenadiers of his own division would reach him on 4th February. The wisdom of thinning out opposite X Corps was confirmed when it was learned on the evening of 2nd February that 56th Infantry Division had left X Corps for Anzio.

By the evening of 2nd February, the US 2nd/135th Infantry had occupied most of the area of gullies and spurs called Colle Maiola. They had shelled 2nd/132rd Grenadiers until they were 'pulverised' and 2nd/361st Panzer Grenadiers until they 'melted like butter in the sun'. Only thirty-two men survived the ordeal and they scratched some shelter in the area of Point 593, hoping to hold out until 3rd Parachute arrived to stop the rot. Battalions caught in the open on those rocky hillsides were quickly destroyed. If the Americans could maintain their momentum it seemed that they must sweep Baade's men off the south-western edge of the Cassino massif.

But during the night the parachutists counterattacked from the area of Point 593, and although they again lost the spur containing the Point 475 and 476 features after recapturing it, they retained the ridge opposite it which led down towards the Monastery and which included Points 450 and 445. On Castellone the US 3rd/135th pushed on to Point 706, while two battalions of the 142nd held the higher feature behind them against attacks from the north. But 1st/361st arrived to hold Point 593, and the parachutists were based on the Albaneta area as a reserve behind 1st Alpine Battalion who now faced 3rd/135th Infantry. The fighting had already reduced the parachutists to 130 men.

When the Parachute Machine Gun Battalion and 1st Parachute were on the way to Cassino, Vietinghoff decided that the whole of the Parachute Division should be brought in by degrees from the Adriatic and that Baade's 90th Division should replace them there. The shattered 2nd/361st was the first to be pulled out. But instead of going to the Adriatic it found itself helping to relieve units of the 44th Division Group so that they could be reorganised. The other battalions of 361 Panzer Grenadiers suffered the same fate. By 4th February the nine battalions of the 44th, two of 8th Panzer Grenadier Regiment and an Alpine company numbered less than 1,500 men.

4th and 5th February were wet and stormy days on which a lull in American activity seemed to indicate that they were at last tiring. Baade's position, on the other hand, was improving. The 1st Parachute celebrated its arrival by pushing 3rd/135th

Cassino comes under long range American artillery fire

Refugees flee from the Cassino area

Infantry off Point 706, but lost it soon after to a counterattack. In what was to be called the Snakeshead Ridge area, the German positions along the ridge containing Points 445 and 450 and around Point 593 began to harden. 1st/200th Panzer Grenadiers, part of the Behr group from Anzio, reached Roccasecca and, soon after, went into reserve behind the Colle Sant' Angelo. Some of the parachute machine gunners took up positions near the Monastery and others joined the hard-pressed 211th Grenadiers in the northern outskirts of Cassino town, where they were located on the mountainside near Point 175, at Point 165 and on Castle Hill.

The US 133rd Infantry took up the running on the 5th. Having previously reached the outlying houses of the town on the road from Monte Villa, they sliced through the machine gunners on Point 175 and briefly occupied Castle Hill. The Castle, separated by a deep gulley from Point 175, was to be a tactical position of great importance in the struggle ahead, but the Americans were not strong enough to hold it.

The lull on top of the hill was required to allow the US 168th Infantry to relieve the 135th opposite the Point 450-445 ridge, six or seven hundred yards from the Monastery itself. The 135th would then concentrate on the

thrust from Snakeshead to Point 593 and Albaneta after its 3rd Battalion had been pulled off the Castellone ridge. The weak 141st and 143rd would then reinforce the 142nd to allow 36th Division to concentrate in the area from Castellone to Massa Manna.

Battalions took three hours to climb to the forward positions and several days to become oriented to a new type of fighting and new terrain. From their caravans miles away on the other side of the Rapido, the divisional and corps staffs could easily lose touch with the conditions of battalions which had been 'up there' a week or more. They knew, as a staff statistic, that the turn-round time of a mule column was about fourteen hours, but not, perhaps, what proportion of the food, blankets, batteries and ammunition was lost on the hillside on the way up, and what the lack entailed for attacking battalions. The commanders, daunted by the length of the journey on foot and the time it took, did not often visit battalions and regiments. In consequence, they were inclined to plan operations from the map without properly grasping the importance of particular features or the peculiar nature of the terrain.

Loss of communication with the fighting units led rear staffs to look at the short distance on the ground which separated their men from the edge of the Monte Cassino massif and to assume that they were as close to victory. Yet their divisions were growing weaker while Baade's original battalions, tired and almost decimated too, were being continually reinforced by fresh units. The US Army was short of reserves in Italy, and was traditionally reluctant to break up organisations to provide fresh battalions, as the Germans had done. The employment of British troops from 46th Division was a possibility, although it raised many administrative problems and the touchy question of the employment of troops of one nationality under the divisional command of another. But when all is said, there is no indication that Keyes or Ryder was prepared to lay down the torch or to accept help from outside the corps to carry it further.

The arrival of the 168th Infantry brought the fighting to a new level of bitterness. When the 34th Division attacked again on the 6th, the battle soon lost even the little coherence it had had before. Telephone cables laid on rocky hillsides were cut by shellfire and the frozen fingers of frightened men were slow to find and splice the breaks. Messengers were despatched, never to be seen again. Radio batteries went dead, charging motors were destroyed and replacements were blown over the edge of tracks, together with mules and attendants. Artillery fire plans were arranged and postponed, then changed and finally cancelled because the battalion going into the assault had not arrived; or had been so weakened by continuous shelling that the men would not rise from their sangars to face an even chance of dying alone from a wound somewhere out in front.

Cold, damp, sleeplessness and incessant noise made the teeth chatter uncontrollably. Hot food never reached the men on forward slopes. Trenchfoot, a cold numbness which, if ignored, made the limb a blue-green gangrenous and useless lump, became common. Officers manned police posts to stop the trickle of walking wounded and stretcher bearers becoming a flood of stragglers looking for relief.

What really happened in that last week of hell behind the Monastery may never be known. The units' reports of their attempts, successes and failures are not always borne out by those of their opponents. For battalion and company commanders knew when the limit of their men's endurance had been reached, even if the staff did not.

It does not seem that attacks along Monte Castellone were ever pressed over the col to the Colle Sant' Angelo. But the 142nd reached Albaneta on the 11th and only the intervention of Oberst Schulz, who committed a platoon of engineers until he could organise a force from his 200th Panzer Grenadier Regiment from behind Points 505 and 575, saved the position. Meanwhile, the terrifying *nebelwerfers* from the 71st Regiment caught a company of the 142nd on the forward slopes of Phantom Ridge and on the ground in front of the ruined abbey and the farm. Few of them returned.

Castellone was a sinister feature – scrubby trees and bushes grew on the three ring contours, but elsewhere there was little shelter. Daylight movement brought immediate retribution from the artillery observers of both sides. The rocks splintered and had as much power to kill and maim as the metal of shells and bombs. Yet it was a highway to the Colle Sant' Angelo ridge, and if sufficient strength could have been found it provided a route straight to the rear of the German positions.

Baade recognised the threat and had been waiting to mount a two-pronged counterattack, operation MICHAEL, since 5th February. The left thrust was to cut through to Terelle and bring the reverse slopes of Snakeshead and Maiola under direct fire. The right was to retake Snakeshead and roll up the Point 475 ridge from the north. Early in the morning of the 12th, Baade at last had a battalion of the 200th Panzer Grenadiers ready for the left thrust, but he had to forego the other. The Grenadiers, it seems, got right to the end of the ridge, meeting little opposition, but they were so heavily shelled all the way that the battalion lost eight officers and 160 men and had to be pulled back. From then until May, when the Poles used this route with final success but initial failure, Castellone saw no important fighting.

More bitter and continuous was the fighting for the positions immediately behind the Monastery. The German defences on Points 569, 593, 450-445, Monastery Hill, and 444 were arranged round the rim of a bowl. When one position was lost it could be counterattacked from another point on the rim. The strongpoints were not reinforced by concrete or panther turrets, as were the ones in the town. But caves in Monastery Hill and behind Point 593 provided shelter for reserves and aid posts. Anti-personnel mines were used effectively, particularly in front of the 450-445 ridge. The defenders learned from experience to cover every dangerous approach with machine gun fire. Gradually, they strengthened their sangars, as the number of their dead and wounded mounted from incessant mortar and artillery fire and strafing fighter-bombers, of which they complained bitterly. But they did not measure their casualties in hundreds like the attackers. It is remarkable that although 'the head' of Snakeshead ridge was higher by a few feet than Point 593, and the other American firm bases were higher than Point 450, the German defences were hidden on the reverse slopes. In contrast the forward American positions were exposed.

The Americans could take only two routes to the German positions. They could move along the narrow and closely observed ridge of Snakeshead to Point 593, the highest point on the rim, and by Points 569, 476 and 444 to the Monastery; or from the 475-474 ridge, across the grain of the country to Point 450-445, and from there across a deep gulley to the Monastery.

The 135th won and lost the summit of Point 593 several times between 6th and 9th February and ultimately American sangars were built within forty yards of the Germans on the top. So close were the two sides that it was not possible to shell Point 593 with safety. In the spring of 1944 green shrubs grew among the boulders and screes – an oasis in a sea of death and destruction.

The 168th launched three great attacks by the other route to the Monastery. They held Point 450-445 only briefly and had to be content with some uncomfortable platoon positions in the gully below it. One of their attacks flowed over Point 445 and down to the foot of Point 516, the hill on which the Monastery stood. They winkled some prisoners out of the caves up on the road but fierce machine gun fire from Points 444 and 476 in the rear, as well as from further along Monastery Hill, forced them to withdraw.

By the end of the 9th, both sides were exhausted. Rain and snow storms on the 10th added to the misery of the men. In one last effort, General Ryder brought the 141st up on to Snakeshead to throw them against Point 593. But their attack was never organised. The 142nd, sent alone against Albaneta, had little chance even though they surprised the defence.

On the 12th, II Corps had to admit that it could do no more. The 135th, with rifle companies down to an average of thirty, were still losing men from shells and sickness even in reserve. The 168th companies may have averaged sixty. The 36th Division had started the battle in a weak state. By the end its battalions were little more than a hundred strong. Down in the Rapido valley, the 133rd Regiment had been attacking 211th Grenadier Regiment incessantly. It, too, was exhausted.

But statistics are inadequate to describe the condition of these divisions. Shells are not respecters of individuals. The brave men and the key men seem to receive more than their share of wounds and death; companies are demoralised by the removal of experienced and trusted officers and NCO's. Battalions are unbalanced when companies have to amalgamate because of casualties. They will recover with rest and reinforcement, but only if an experienced nucleus has survived and with it the sense of having fought stoutly and effectively.

Frightful though their casualties were, the 34th did leave the hill proudly. Fred Majdalany, a company commander in the British 78th Infantry Division which fought at Cassino later, wrote this of them:

'The performance of the 34th Division at Cassino must rank with the finest feats of arms carried out by any soldiers during the war. When at last they were relieved by the 4th Indian Division fifty of those few who had held on to the last were too numbed with cold exhaustion to move. They could still man their positions but they could not move out of them unaided. They were carried out on stretchers . . .'

A few days later, another National Guard division, the 45th, was earning the grudging respect of the Germans at Anzio.

The torch is passed

While the desperate struggle in the mountains was dragging on, the 4th Indian Division concentrated behind II Corps for the *coup de grace*. It was to form an improvised corps with 2nd New Zealand Division. The New Zealanders provided the corps staff; additional supply units, engineers and an army group Royal Artillery were added for logistical and fire support.

In the Indian division there was some residual experience of mountain fighting from the North West Frontier, the Keren Campaign in 1941 and from Tunisia. But the division had not trained, neither was it equipped, to fight in the mountains. It had too few mules, only about 900, under French, American and Indian control. Like all British divisions, it was poorly supplied with four-wheel drive vehicles. The 5th and 7th Indian Brigades had joined the Eighth Army only in December 1943 and had fought on that front for two weeks in January. The 11th had been only recently reformed. It was destroyed in the Tobruk disaster in June, 1942 and had not fought with the division since. Therefore

4th Indian and 2nd NZ Divisions take up the torch – for the *coup de grace*?

Veteran NZ General Bernard Freyberg

while 4th Indian had a proud tradition, a formidable reputation, although it contained many veterans, and was fresh and eager to do well, it was not a battle-hardened divisional team.

Each brigade of the division included one British battalion. The two Indian Army battalions were commanded by British officers with a unique system of British and Indian King's Commissioned Officers and Indian Viceroy's Commissioned Officers under them. The Indian divisions were highly professional. They were also very intimate, almost family affairs, in which bold leadership by the officers was expected and could produce a brilliant response. Equally, casualties, fatigue and failure in that quarter were sometimes reflected in inertia and apathy in the men. But after these general remarks, it must be said also that the battalions from the Indian sub-continent each reflected the particular strengths and weaknesses of the peoples from which they were recruited.

Something of the feeling of officers for their men can be understood from a passage in a letter written to General Freyberg by the divisional general, F I S Tuker, who was taken ill just before the Cassino battle: 'I am ever so thankful my division is being looked after by yourself. With you there, I know that no single life will be squandered and that those that are spent will be well spent.'

The 2nd New Zealand Division was also a family affair. The veteran Lieutenant-General Bernard Freyberg, who had been a very young divisional commander in the First World War and had probably seen more action than any other commander on either side in the Second, presided over it. A posting to his division was considered an honour. The places of those who were unsatisfactory could easily be filled and more than one member of the division had refused to be promoted because it meant leaving.

The divisional organisation was unusual in that it contained two infantry brigades and one armoured brigade. For this reason Alexander had envisaged using 2nd New Zealand Division for the mobile operations which might follow a breach of the Gustav Line. But it was also strong enough in infantry to conduct the break-in and dog-fight phases, provided they were not too protracted.

When Mark Clark committed the New Zealand Corps he directed it to break out into the Liri valley as well as to capture Cassino. His requirement influenced the ensuing battles in inhibiting the commanders from committing troops early in the fight lest they had insufficient for the breakout.

The German offensive at Anzio, actually resumed on 16th February, had a more immediate and malignant influence. In anticipation of it, the New Zealand Corps was ordered to continue the attack at Cassino to pin German units in the Gustav Line without delay. Consequently, Freyberg was not allowed time to let his divisions settle down. The 4th Indian Division suffered seriously from lack of time. Because of the mule shortage

A New Zealand anti-tank gun crew in action below Cassino

most of 11th Indian Brigade had to be used as carriers. Even with the assistance of American trucks to bring supplies forward to the road-head east of the Rapido, their supply of grenades and mortar bombs was notoriously inadequate when the attack opened. And both were key weapons in mountain fighting.

Consequently, no one was enthusiastic at New Zealand Corps' Headquarters over the condition under which the battle was to begin. Yet, if 34th Division had had Baade's men rocking on their heels, there was much to be said for resuming the offensive before they had recovered.

The peculiar status of 2nd New Zealand Division was another factor which may have affected the conduct of the coming battles. Under special circumstances and in grave emergency the charter given to Freyberg by the New Zealand government permitted him to refuse to accept assignments given to his division. Under the conditions existing in February, when the fate of VI Corps was in the balance, this implied only that Freyberg might be expected to ensure that his division was committed under the most favourable conditions possible. But it also meant that Clark, an American, was unlikely to insist that the battle be continued until the division was in danger of being destroyed. Clark would be particularly careful, as he had been with the British troops under his command, that his relations with the New Zealanders remained amicable. He would tend to ride Freyberg on a light rein.

On the evening of 11th February, Major-General Gruenther, Fifth Army's Chief of Staff, phoned Freyberg. 'The torch is now thrown to you', he said. It was not the first or the last time that that had happened to the New Zealanders or to the 4th Indian Division. Clark ordered the 133rd Infantry to remain in the northern outskirts of Cassino to assist the

General Baade, sector commander, Cassino

New Zealand Corps.

On the same day, Alexander had directed Fifth Army to continue, without delay, the attack on the hill with 4th Indian Division and simultaneously to seize a bridgehead over the Rapido near the town. However, the breakout was not to be attempted unless the ground had dried sufficiently to allow armour to operate off the roads. The attack was planned for the night of 12th February.

On examining the ground near the river, the New Zealanders found that not even infantry could operate satisfactorily over it, let alone their support weapons or tanks. Consequently, successive postponements of the attack became necessary until the standing water had dispersed. On the hill there were also delays. The 7th Indian Brigade was to relieve the 135th, 168th and 141st Infantry in the Snakeshead area while the rest of 36th Division remained on Castellone.

But when the brigade moved up on the night of 11th February, it ran into 200th Panzer Grenadier Regiment's operation MICHAEL against Monte Castellone. Throughout the following day it scratched defensive positions behind 36th Division and suffered casualties from shelling at the rate of twenty an hour. The relief of the forward units on Snakeshead began that night but was not completed until first light on the 14th. Two more days passed before 7th Brigade was properly organised on top of the hill and 5th Brigade was in position behind them.

The New Zealand Corps had found it difficult to discover the exact location of the Americans from staff officers at II Corps' Headquarters. Brigadier Kippenberger, who had succeeded Freyberg in command of 2nd New Zealand Division, may not have been pointing his finger unfairly when he wrote that he attended a conference at II Corps at which Freyberg 'questioned the American commanders closely as to the condition of their troops and it was very plain that none of them had been forward or was at all in touch with his men . . .'

When the 1st Battalion of the Royal Sussex took over the Snakeshead area on the night of 12th February it was discovered that the 135th Infantry was not astride Point 593 as II Corps had stated. Neither were the Americans in control of the Point 450-445 ridge but were in the gullies 200 yards below it. The Germans controlled the ridge. Four hundred yards beyond it the Monastery glowered at them from the other side of another deep gully with caves and out crops of rock on its far slopes. Lieutenant-Colonel J Glennie, the Commanding Officer of 1st Royal Sussex, noted in his diary for 12th February: 'I was guided up to the sector by an American guide, who led me toward the German positions until we were fired on. After a hasty retreat, the American position was approached from the enemy side! On arrival it was found that the sector was held by four US battalions (now

Amici italiani,

ATTENZIONE!

Noi abbiamo sinora cercato in tutti i modi di evitare il bombardamento del monastero di Montecassino. I tedeschi hanno saputo trarre vantaggio da ciò. Ma ora il combattimento si è ancora più stretto attorno al Sacro Recinto. E venuto il tempo in cui a malincuore siamo costretti a puntare le nostre armi contro il Monastero stesso.

Noi vi avvertiamo perché voi abbiate la possibilità di porvi in salvo. Il nostro avvertimento è urgente: Lasciate il Monastero. Andatevene subito. Rispettate questo avviso. Esso è stato fatto a vostro vantaggio.

LA QUINTA ARMATA.

Italian friends,

BEWARE!

We have until now been especially careful to avoid shelling the Monte Cassino Monastery. The Germans have known how to benefit from this. But now the fighting has swept closer and closer to its sacred precincts. The time has come when we must train our guns on the Monastery itself.

We give you warning so that you may save yourselves. We warn you urgently: Leave the Monastery. Leave it at once. Respect this warning. It is for your benefit.

THE FIFTH ARMY.

12th February. General Alexander makes the decision to bomb the Monastery

each only 100 strong) of three different regiments of two different divisions.' If it had been possible to feed fresh American units into the battle, instead of replacing American divisions with others which had different equipment and methods, the fighting on the hill might have been continued without a break. The Germans, who were not handicapped by the protocol or the logistic problems of coalition warfare, had done so. But their aim was single – to hold Cassino at all costs. And Kesselring overrode divisional and regimental commanders in other sectors when they objected to being continually milked of units to ensure that Cassino held.

However, in the week between 9th and 16th February Baade managed to strengthen his position not by reinforcements but by improving field works and ammunition supplies. Indeed he reported that I/361 and II/3 Parachute and the Parachute Machine Gun Battalion were 'used up' and that III/361 and II/1 Parachute were badly battered. 'Used up' meant that their overall strength was reduced to less than 100 men and 'badly battered' to about 150. But 200th Panzer Grenadier Regiment, despite heavy casualties in operation MICHAEL, was still in good condition and Knuth's 211 Grenadiers, the defenders of the northern approaches to the town, had covered themselves with glory and been cited. Given a few more days respite the defenders would survive until 4th Parachute Regiment arrived on 19th February. By the 23rd the whole of the Parachute Division would be at Cassino and General Heidrich would take Baade's place as sector commander.

On 16th February, hardly a regiment of XIV Panzer Corps, let alone a division, had all its troops under command in one sector. But between the 13th and 15th, 29th Panzer Grenadier Division was reunited at Anzio

The Abbot and General von Senger

so that the elements of 71st Infantry Division and 15th Panzer Grenadiers which were fighting there could return to their formations in XIV Corps. This Greek gift strengthened the Fourteenth Army but did little to sort out the muddle in the Tenth. For the three regiments of the 71st would have to be disposed from Castelforte, opposite X Corps in the south, to Belmonte, in the north. The golden exception to the muddle was to be at Cassino where the Parachute Division would be concentrated. But a crucial week lay ahead before Heidrich's men could take over there.

Freyberg wrote the plan for the New Zealand Corps' Operation AVENGER on 9th February when it became clear that the Americans were exhausted. Behind the Monastery the Indians were to continue where the Americans had left off. But down in the valley, the New Zealanders would attack on the left of Route 6 to avoid the centre of Cassino town. They would follow the line of the railway embankment, cross the river and seize the railway station. In the second phase they would thrust into the area of the Roman Theatre. At thè southern entrance to the town they would consolidate the road junction at which Route 6 turned to the north-west up the Liri valley towards Piedimonte. Meanwhile, the Indians would have come down from the Monastery to join them on Route 6. The defenders of the town would then be surrounded.

The New Zealanders' main problem was to clear ten demolitions in the railway embankment on both sides of the river and to bridge the Rapido and its branches so that the embankment could be used for wheeled and tracked vehicles. The embankment provided the only dry axis over the river and the Germans had been thorough and imaginative in blocking it. Lieutenant Faram of 5th New Zealand Field Park Company reported on one of them: 'Demolition 7 (86501933) – bridge over Rapido blown – 78 feet gap 8 feet deep – Messerschmidt 109 in gap – can be forded – hard gravel bottom – doze down each side.' The problem, as with all river crossings, was to build the class 9 and class 40 bridges quickly so that the support weapons and tanks could move into the bridgehead. The infantry had to protect the engineers from small arms fire and the sniping assault-guns using direct fire. They had to expect and endure shellfire.

The situation behind the Monastery was less happy. Brigadier Dimoline, the Commander Royal Artillery of 4th Indian Division, had to deputise for the sick Tuker although the General remained in the background trying to ensure that his division attacked with every advantage. Brigadier O de T Lovett, who commanded 7th Brigade, reconnoitred with Glennie at Snakeshead on the 12th. Afterwards they convinced Dimoline that Point 593 had to be taken as a firm base before the Monastery could be attacked. Next day, when the Royal Sussex were settling in, Freyberg agreed that the first priority should be the firm base and that the time element was of secondary importance. By that he meant that the main attack was to be on the night of the 16th which he believed would satisfy Alexander's need for speed.

Glennie had found general agreement among Americans up the hill that the Monastery was being used by the Germans. The 168th Infantry had evidence that there were posts in the caves and among the rocks below Point 516. It was naïve to believe that German company commanders had not made use of the shelters on such a valuable backstop despite any orders they may have received to the contrary. Sensible battalion commanders, told to respect the sanctity of the Monastery, would not expect their company commanders to include in the order the hill on which it stood. Even today, the contention that posts circled the Monastery only at a distance of 400 metres cannot be taken seriously. Each of the German

positions at Point 236 above the top bend on the road from the town, Point 435 called Hangman's Hill, and Point 445 was closer than that.

The consensus of opinion on 12th February, 1944 was that victory in the coming battle would be prejudiced if the Monastery were not bombed. It was argued that the building could not be respected because the feature on which it stood was part of the German defence system. That fact, at least, was not in dispute, even if there was doubt as to whether the Monastery itself was being used. Nothing in the operational directives issued by superior headquarters decreed that ancient monuments should be spared at the price of men's lives. Indeed, how could such a principle be expressed but by the warning that wanton destruction was the real crime against civilisation? And Montecassino, the Mother House of the Benedictine Order, might be the largest ancient building ever to be deliberately destroyed, but it was not the first, nor

The controversial bombing and shelling of the 1,400-year old Monastery. The Germans were not actually inside

the most beautiful. The Monastery had suffered violence many times in the 1,400 years since it was established. And a thousand years before St Benedict was born, a menacing Etruscan citadel had squatted on top of the hill where the Monastery now stood.

Kesselring had discussed the status of the Monastery when the defences of the Gustav Line were being planned. He did not forbid Tenth Army to use the Abbey grounds but only insisted that its men must not enter the building. In fact, as the Benedictine Order owned the land for miles around, he made the only practical distinction which could be made. The Führer gave orders at the end of December that Montecassino was to be 'included in the defence line and to be fortified.' However, the evidence indicates that the buildings were excluded from the

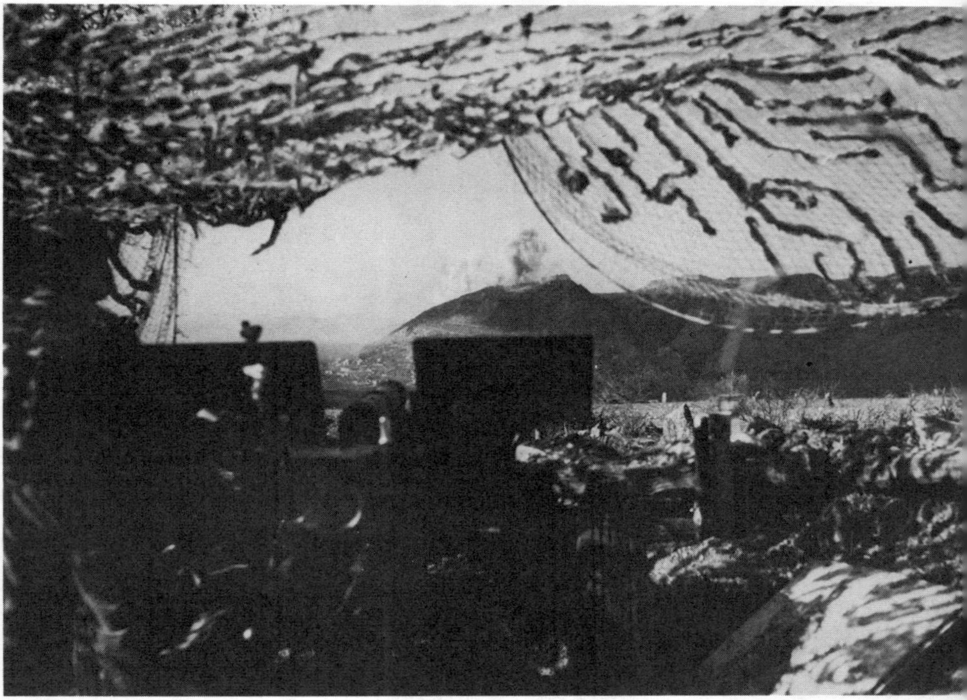

defences although they mght have been useful to shelter reserves, supplies, headquarters and medical units, and for observation. On the other hand, it was generally believed by American units that this sort of use had been made of them.

The implications of making a distinction between the building and the ground were not pursued while the decision to bomb the Monastery was being hammered out on 12th February. Clark was absent for most of that day at Anzio and he used Gruenther to explain his objections to it. His statement that the commanders of II Corps and 34th and 36th Divisions did not consider the bombing necessary, cannot have impressed Freyberg for he knew that their own men on the hill thought otherwise. But Clark's contention that the Monastery in ruins would be no less an obstacle was answered by Freyberg's contention that the occupants would be stunned and that the ruined Monastery could be overrun before they could recover. An alternative – that of treating the known localities on its north side as a legitimate target and allowing the Monastery to take its chance, which would have been in line with both the usages of war and the realities of the German defences – was not seriously considered. Even after the withdrawal of a number of forward posts, it would have required greater accuracy by the heavy bombers than they could command to avoid accidents. Whereas no bomb aimer, it seemed, could miss the Monastery. This belief was shortlived.

Clark was opposed to the bombing, but he was not prepared to deny the New Zealanders and 4th Indian Division even the psychological advantage of seeing that 'hateful tapestry' torn from the skyline. But he would not accept the odium of giving the order either and he asked General Alexander to make the final decision. With Alexander's acquiescence on the evening of 12th February the planning went ahead on the

Left: **Despite the bombing and shelling, the Germans hold Cassino.** ***Above:*** **General Heidrich, soon to take over from Baade, the victor of this round**

assumption that the bombing would be part of 4th Indian Division's fireplan.

Dimoline wanted to attack Point 593 on the night of 15th February. He visualised the Monastery being bombed late on the 16th. His main attack would be made that night after a temporary withdrawal behind a bombline. On the 14th, leaflets warned the Germans and the civilians inside the Monastery that the time had come when the Allies had regretfully to train their guns on the place. The actual time when this would happen was not mentioned, although the monks were urged to evacuate the Monastery immediately.

The timing of the bombing would normally have depended simply on the readiness of 5th and 7th Brigades to attack and on the suitability of the weather. But it was understood that as the aircraft might no longer be available after the German offensive opened at Anzio, the Monastery had to be bombed on the first fine day even

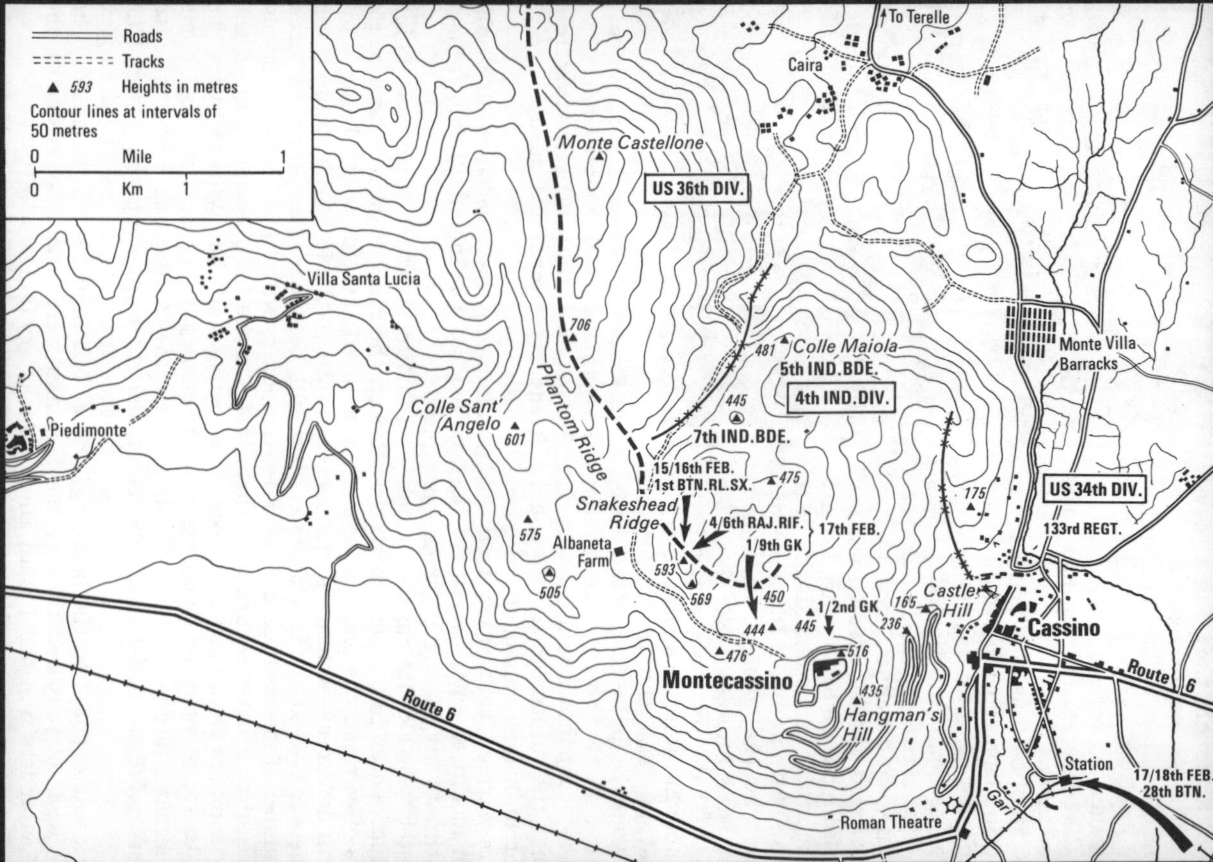

The torch is passed, but 4th Indian Division makes little progress towards Montecassino (15th/17th February)

if 4th Indian Division was not ready. Yet Dimoline was taken by surprise when Freyberg informed him on the evening of 14th February that the bombing must take place the next morning. The forecast for the 15th was 'fair at first, risk of rain tomorrow'. It was now or never, he was told. He was to decide within half an hour whether to commit his division to attack unprepared in the wake of the bombers or after the shock effect on the enemy had worn off on the 16th, as planned. Freyberg also wanted to know if he could withdraw his forward troops 1,000 yards as he had planned to do if the bombing had taken place on the 16th.

Dimoline was forced to conclude that he could neither mount an attack next morning nor withdraw his troops in time.

At 0930 hours on the 15th the bombing started. Somehow, brigade headquarters received only a few seconds notice of it. The units received none. 'They told the monks and they told the enemy but they didn't tell us,' wrote Glennie whose battalion received a few overs on Snakeshead.

The German High Command Communiqué for 15th February stated that the 'world famous Abbey of Cassino' had been attacked and badly damaged by enemy bombers, although there was not one German soldier either in the building or in the immediate vicinity. Next day it announced that the ruins had been 'incorporated into the German defence front.' But before the Goebbels propaganda machinery had changed into top gear, Westphal and Wentzell discussed 'the Monastery affair' on the telephone. The latter described it as 'a bad business'. 'But does it do us any harm from a military point of view?' asked Westphal. 'No, because we were not inside. They only made out that we were', Wentzell replied. The two men then dropped the subject and went on to discuss logistical problems of ammunition supply.

The attacks launched by 5th and 7th Brigades caused Oberst Schulz's units behind the Monastery little concern. On the other hand, the four battalions which attacked them suffered heavily. The bombing of the Monastery did not help them at all. In three nights of fighting nearly forty officers and 600 men were killed, wounded or missing.

The reason for the failure is not hard to determine. The defenders had been provided with an abundant supply of hand grenades and the dischargers with which they could be launched from the safety of sangars. It was not until the first week of March that similar launchers arrived for the Indians, despite repeated demands. The Germans had developed minebelts, particularly along the Point 450-445 ridge, and had used their experience in the hectic days of early February to coordinate machine gun tasks more closely. The only approaches were registered by mortars and there was plenty of ammunition.

Snakeshead ridge was so narrow that a battalion could not deploy on more than a company front for an assault on Point 593. In an effort to bring more men to bear, a Royal Sussex company tried to attack Point 593 from the north but was stopped by a ravine. Some of the men who reached its summit from the other side fell over a cliff in the dark. Local knowledge from patrols and daylight observation might have prevented these mishaps. But the Americans, who might have informed the Royal Sussex about the terrain and the German positions, had been driven off their positions directly under the summit of Point 593. Many of those who had been in the close-quarters fighting in the first days of February were either in hospital or dead. Over one hundred American and German corpses lay out on Snakeshead alone. Most of them were still there at the end of February.

After the failure of the preliminary attempts to take Point 593, first with a company on the night of the 15th and then with the whole of the Royal

Sussex on the next night, an attack was launched on a broader front. Battalions of both 5th brigade and 7th Brigade attempted to occupy the whole defensive bowl including the Monastery. 1st/9th Gurkhas attacked over the shoulder of Point 593 directly towards Point 444, after the 4th/6th Rajputana Rifles had been launched against Point 593 on their right. At the same time, the 1st/2nd Gurkhas, attacking from the direction of Point 476, tried to overrun Point 450 and roll on down to the foot of Monastery Hill.

Although the artillery could not support the attacks effectively because of the proximity of the German positions, small groups of Rajputanas reached the top of Point 593 and 1st/9th Gurkhas penetrated even as far as Point 444, while some sections of the 1st/2nd Gurkhas bombed their way along the Point 450 ridge. But a thorn thicket near the crest of Point 450, unexpectedly buttressed with Schu and S mines, and laced with machine gun fire, prevented most of the Gurkhas from closing with the main German positions on the reverse slope. Those who succeeded were blasted by the fire from the Monastery and the ridge between it and Point 569.

As the position of those still forward would have been hopeless in daylight, the survivors were pulled back. The 1st/2nd Gurkhas held the forward slope of the 450-445 ridge and the Rajputanas hung on just under the top of Point 593. These new positions were not tactically advantageous but they were occupied until the division was relieved in March. No more attempts to turn the German flank behind the Monastery were made until the Polish Corps attacked in May.

'It was repeatedly emphasized', wrote Lieutenant-Colonel Glennie in his diary on 16th February, 'that something must be done to take the pressure off the Anzio beachhead which was in imminent danger of collapse.' It was also the opinion of Alexander and Clark that as the Americans had nearly succeeded, the attack ought to be resumed before the Germans could recover. In consequence, units which had so far always been successful and which were 'not given to bellyaching', attacked before they had seen oblique photographs of the objectives, with only twelve bombs for each 2-inch mortar, sufficient grenades for only one company in each battalion and poorly planned artillery support.

The insistence on speed was not based on sound military reasoning. Clearly, VI Corps would have been best served by a breakthrough at Cassino. The Germans would not have weakened their defences opposite the New Zealand Corps to strengthen Anzio while the danger of one existed. Once an attack started it would have been too late to do so. Only if it failed might they be able to thin out their front. Therefore the time factor ought not to have been the decisive factor which forced the 4th Indian Division into a premature attack.

The decision to make them attack before they were ready is curious in the light of Alexander's statement that he did not intend the exploitation phase of AVENGER to proceed unless the ground was dry. A breakthrough to Anzio was not intended. Therefore the bad timing which marked the decision to commit the US 36th Infantry in January was repeated with 4th Indian Division. The same unsophisticated reasoning, that Fifth Army must keep attacking to save Anzio, was evident.

Tactical surprise could not be obtained behind the Monastery. Therefore, if Anzio had not been allowed to dominate command thinking the time of the attack would have been determined by the rate of build-up of the Indians' supplies and the state of their Intelligence. Their opponents had already had seven days to improve their defences; further delay would have benefited the Indians rather than the defence. In particular, the artillery would have had time to master the difficult problems of crest clearance and shooting from a flank, and the mortars could have built up their supply. The defenders were not protected by concrete and steel as has sometimes been said, but by stone sangars which were merely better constructed than those which the Indians took over from the attacking Americans. The Germans were vulnerable to accurate fire, although not to the same extent as the attackers.

Surprise might have been obtained by attacking immediately after the bombing. But as General Freyberg could not coordinate the air and ground attacks because of the demands of Anzio, the bombing was tactically irrelevant. When the Germans occupied the ruins the results were positively harmful, and not a bonus as had been hoped. Mark Clark was correct in this forecast. Yet the troops on the ground insisted that had they been ready they could have rushed the Monastery before the Germans recovered from their shock. However, that seems unlikely because the German defences were not at the mean point of impact.

The New Zealanders' attack on the railway station came nearer to success. But they, too, were forced into tactics which put them at a disadvantage. They had to attack at night on a front of only one battalion because of the floods, and the reinforcing battalions with support weapons and tanks had to be pumped in over the viaduct soon after dawn to maintain the momentum of the assault. The defence was to be distracted by feint attacks and a bombardment by support weapons in the northern outskirts of the town to conceal the location of the *schwerpunkt*. But this distraction would not deceive the defence for long.

After the assault on the railway station by Lieutenant-Colonel Young's Maoris of 28th Battalion had succeeded, everything depended on the engineers. They would have to start to bridge the tributary of the Rapido, the main stream and then a tributary of the Gari and repair four other demolitions on the railway line with bulldozers while the Maoris were advancing. If they completed their work in the hours of darkness, Lieutenant-Colonel McGaffin's 19th Armoured Regiment would pass over the causeway and into the station with 23rd Battalion. Most of this force would exploit to the southern outskirts of the town while the rest joined the defenders of the station area to pin down the Germans in the centre of the town.

H-hour was 2130 hours on the 17th but the companies arrived late at the start line, muddy and soaked to the skin. The objectives were shelled until H+10 and then the guns switched to counterbattery tasks and targets on the flanks. At the beginning, the two leading companies, stumbling through drainage ditches and wet fields to the left of the embankment, ran into uncleared mines and they were soon being heavily mortared. On the right, B Company took two hours to reach the German defences. Then, after a moment of hesitation, two men ran forward, lay on the wire, and the rest of the platoon ran over them and into the attack as if negotiating an assault course. Two posts of 3rd/361st Panzer Grenadiers guarding the station were overrun with the bayonet. The wire which guarded them was cut and the rest of the company streamed through the gap. Captain Wikiriwhi's men had the station buildings and the round house in their hands by midnight, but they could not take their second objective, some houses beyond the station, because A Company was held up by a deep tributary of the Gari which was protected by wire and mines. Behind it, a hummock just south of the Round House was strongly held. By dawn the two forward companies were therefore held up. Their future depended on the progress of the engineers behind them.

Work on the causeway had fallen behind schedule. A platoon which was working on a thirty-foot bridge over the Rapido backwater had taken

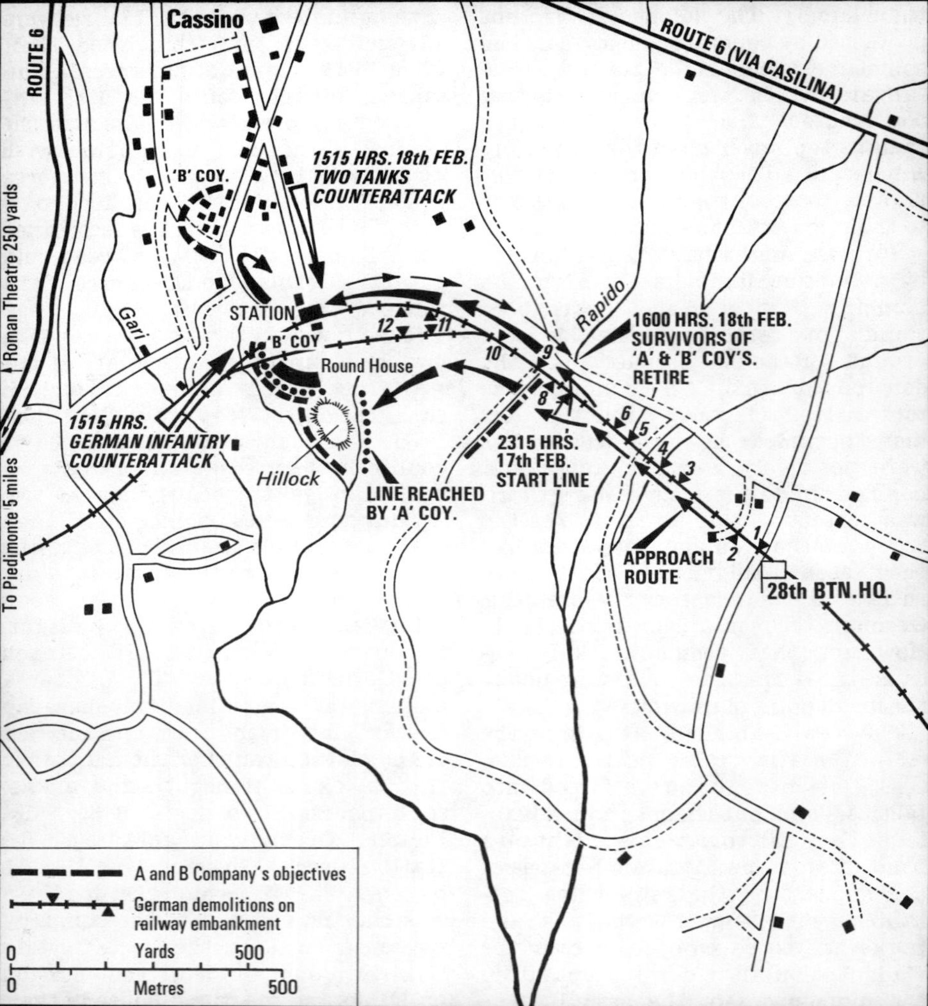

Operation Avenger: 28th Battalion (Maoris), 5th New Zealand Brigade attacks Cassino station

cover from the shelling and been hindered by the passage of 28th Battalion as it moved forward to the start line between 2030 and 2130 hours. Instead of opening at 2100 hours the bridge was not ready until 2315. The lost time was never made up. It was 0500 hours before the main bridge was completed and by then the engineers were five hours behind their timetable. Even by leap-frogging working parties, demolitions 11 and 12 still blocked the passage of vehicles into the station at dawn. After that, despite gallant examples set by individuals, the divisional engineers were not ordered to persevere.

At sunrise the counterattacks began. For a time, smoke hid the Maoris from their opponents and high explosive defensive fires broke up the German attacks. But when Young sent a reinforcing platoon over the river, it suffered twelve casualties and never reached the station. The field regiment responsible for the smoke screen which hid them fired 9,000 rounds during 18th January. Despite a crisis over the supply of smoke shells which was surmounted, the early afternoon came with the Maoris still in the station. The combined efforts of 3rd/361st and 211th Grenadiers had failed to remove them.

At about 1515 hours, the last available German reserves were thrown in along the railway line while two tanks closed in from the north. Through heavy defensive fire the latter muscled their way into the station yard. The 28th Battalion's anti-tank guns had been unable to cross the river and the Maoris had no more PIAT ammunition. The defence cracked. At 1600 hours the survivors staggered back across the river. Of the 200 men who started out, only seventy returned. German casualties were slightly greater.

Baade's men had been taken by surprise. The 211th Grenadiers had reported a 'broadfronted attack north of Cassino' while the Maoris were attacking the station. When the station fell Baade switched all his sector artillery to the Rapido bridge, but by 0420 his first-line ammunition holdings were exhausted. By dawn, 3rd/361st had had heavy casualties in the station sector and the further advance of the New Zealanders was prevented only by a scratch force from 211th Grenadiers using the natural strength of the hillock position. The situation appeared worse than it was because New Zealand tanks were reported to have reached the station. Baade believed he could seal off the penetration if his ammunition supply were replenished, but doubted if he could restore the front without help. At this stage he did not yet know that he was fighting New Zealanders.

The final counterattack that won the day was launched by 2nd/8th Panzer Grenadiers which had been rushed round from Terelle with some other unspecified reserves and placed under the command of 211th Grenadiers.

On 22nd February, Senger cited Baade as the victor of Montecassino and awarded him the Oak Leaves to the Knight's Cross. The day before, when Senger visited the sector, the two men had discussed the recent battles and the relative qualities of the Allied troops involved. The New Zealanders were not mentioned, because their toughness was taken for granted, perhaps. But it was noted that the Americans seemed to have lost all their previous reluctance to engage in close combat and if an attack in one area failed they quickly rallied for action elsewhere. By comparison with the more methodical British, who fired only on previously registered targets, the American gunners fired 'uninterruptedly and in all directions' and generally speaking their troops had become 'a very great deal tougher'. The Indians were not as effective as they had once been, were 'flank conscious' and 'avoided close combat'.

Both Senger and Baade expected an early resumption of the battle.

Between rounds

After the battle Kesselring sent his congratulations to Vietinghoff. 'Convey my heartfelt gratitude to 211th Regiment and to 1st Parachute Regiment not quite so strongly. I am very pleased that the New Zealanders have had a smack in the nose. You must recommend the local commander for the Knight's Cross.' Kesselring graduated his praise according to the relative difficulty of the tasks of Schulz opposite the Indians and Knuth who had faced the New Zealanders. The former was never in danger; the latter saved the day when it seemed to be almost lost. Although N C Phillips, the New Zealanders' official historian, wrote that 'New Zealand hopes were dupes and German fears were liars', he believed that the New Zealanders could have won. And he was right.

The New Zealanders were trained to attack on a wide front and then to exploit only successful thrusts. In AVENGER they had had to use a narrow front. Yet they had achieved surprise by simulation. The Germans thought that the main thrust was coming from the north – as it had when the 133rd Infantry attacked in

Anzio beachhead claims more Allied resources as the Germans counterattack

While Truscott and Alexander talk on the Anzio front, Heidrich and Kesselring plan at Cassino

January. But having caught the Germans on the wrong foot, the New Zealanders failed to exploit their initial advantage.

Potentially, the engineers were the weakest link in the chain. It was clear from the beginning that the two assaulting companies would be unable to hold the bridgehead unless supporting weapons could cross the engineers' bridges soon after dawn. On the other hand, if the bridges were built in time, armour could cross them to establish itself at the southern end of the town to seal the fate of the Germans.

In the event, the engineers were poorly led. For it cannot be said that they failed in the face of insuperable difficulties. It is true that when the battle behind the Monastery ended at dawn the Germans switched all their artillery on to the bridge sites. But as their ammunition was rationed they gave the engineers a less unpleasant time than the Maoris a few hundred yards away.

It could be argued that the other rifle companies of 28th Battalion ought to have entered the battle immediately behind A and B Companies; that with their help, the hillock and the houses beyond the station might have been taken. They could have brought forward extra platoon anti-tank weapons. Certainly a larger force would have provided a cushion of time against delays at the bridge. Even granted that the station was only a company-sized defence area, the presence of a reserve in the buildings might have turned the scale. This indication of the commander's intention to hold 28th Battalion's bridgehead might have forced the engineers to continue in daylight, instead of waiting for another night before finishing their task.

This criticism does not depend on hindsight. As success hinged on the engineers, as soon as the leading companies had reached their objectives more infantry should have been sent forward. The plan neither provided for the exploitation of surprise nor for a hedge against the most obvious source of failure.

By the end of 18th February, Mackensen's Anzio offensive down the Albano road from Aprilia had been bloodily repulsed. Truscott replaced Lucas in command of VI Corps a few days later and prepared for a resumption of the struggle. At Cassino, Senger and Baade, the latter about to be succeeded by General Heidrich and his private army of parachutists, were of the same mind about the Allies' intentions at Cassino.

Behind the scenes, the Allies were re-examining their strategy and arguing about the rival claims of OVERLORD, ANVIL, SHINGLE and the Italian campaign in general. The debate occurred in the days immediately following AVENGER and led eventually to the operation in May called DIADEM. But while the implications of it were being worked out, the new strategy and the old co-existed uncomfortably for a little longer. It was during this period of transition that the New Zealand Corps' next operation, DICKENS, was conceived.

DIADEM would require the seizure of a bridgehead in the Liri valley as a springboard. In the meantime, VI Corps continued to be in danger at Anzio, and it was believed that Fifth Army had to maintain the pressure on XIV Panzer Corps to prevent Kesselring from reinforcing Mackensen. Therefore, the New Zealand Corps was ordered to resume its attempt to procure a bridgehead at Cassino and to break out into the Liri valley. The object was to effect a junction with VI Corps; and this remained the object while the DIADEM plan was germinating.

Nevertheless, in Alexander's operations staff an important change in emphasis had already occurred when

American casualties in the air over Cassino (above) and the Anzio beachhead (right)

AVENGER ended. It was now believed that VI Corps would have to exist until the spring before being relieved. The breakout from the Gustav Line would not take place until then. This conception required another examination of the disposal of shipping between the Mediterranean and OVERLORD. For it had once been assumed that the SHINGLE commitment would have ended, Rome would have fallen, and the armies have reached the Pisa-Rimini line, in time to release shipping for OVERLORD and ANVIL in summer 1944.

The British view was that strategic plans which had been agreed even at the highest level ought to be subject to review in the light of experience. The American Chiefs of Staff were inclined to stigmatise British pragmatism either as 'muddling through' or as Machiavellian intrigue. They feared lest the main operation, OVERLORD, should be weakened by prior commitments elsewhere which could not have a decisive effect on the Germans. Originally, they had opposed SHINGLE because they believed it might be the thin end of the

The Americans at Anzio. By 18th February Mackensen's offensive against Allied VI Corps had been bloodily repulsed, but still Fifth Army had to press Cassino to prevent Kesselring reinforcing Mackensen

wedge. And here they were, at the end of February, with the Anglo-American VI Corps still demanding shipping which ought to have been preparing for Normandy. OVERLORD could not be switched on and off like a tap to suit the Italian theatre, they insisted.

General John Harding, Alexander's Chief of Staff, had to agree that SHINGLE had not turned out as planned. On the other hand, if the success of the Allies in Italy was to be measured by German casualties, SHINGLE had been a success. It had forced the Germans to commit reserves and to attack and they had suffered heavily in the process. Therefore, it had already contributed more to the success of OVERLORD than had the slogging winter battles on the main front. Besides, however distasteful, VI Corps was a fact. It had to be maintained and it could yet play an important role in the spring.

It was the gist of Harding's appreciation that to continue to attack in the worst of the winter weather in order to reach Rome, which had no military significance, would so weaken the Allies that they would not be able to use their preponderance of guns and tanks to exploit the unsound German position in the spring. At best, the Germans might be forced to withdraw to cover Rome. If they did so their positions would be sounder than at present and the Allies would be too exhausted to pursue them. On the other hand, if VI Corps and the main front were both strengthened during what remained of the bad weather and the Germans did not withdraw before the spring, a great victory might be attained. A victory would be the best possible contribution to OVERLORD.

Harding concluded that the winter offensive should end and that infantry reinforcements should be sent to the Italian theatre.

The adoption of Harding's proposals would demand a major modification of Allied strategy. Reinforcements would be granted to Alexander very reluctantly. A further disruption of the shipping plan and another threat to ANVIL would be bitterly resisted.

The relentless winter offensive had been made necessary by the timetable imposed by OVERLORD and ANVIL. Now, Alexander was proposing to retain the shipping for SHINGLE until April and to divert infantry reinforcements destined for OVERLORD or ANVIL to reinforce Italy. And since DIADEM was to start only in April the divisions in Italy earmarked for ANVIL would not be available to take part. Furthermore, DIADEM must continue beyond the date for ANVIL, otherwise it would not serve the purpose of attracting German divisions away from OVERLORD. Consequently, Alexander also proposed that there should be only a feint landing in southern France. ANVIL should be cancelled. Better one full-blooded operation than weak efforts in both the south of France and Italy, he argued.

The proposals were soundly based on the explicit and accepted purpose of the Allied armies in Italy – that they were to force the Germans to commit as many divisions to the Italian peninsula as possible by the time OVERLORD was launched. Alexander had assumed that this was best done by inflicting casualties on the enemy. In turn, that required a victory; and the further south it was attained, the worse would be the German losses in their retreat. Therefore, the Germans must be prevented from making a planned withdrawal from the Gustav Line. To ensure a victory, the SHINGLE forces had to be strengthened as well as the main front.

Eisenhower agrees to give priority to Italian operations

The American Chiefs of Staff could not disagree with this reasoning: it was the conclusion that they disliked. But Alexander found an unexpected ally in Eisenhower. Eisenhower's Mediterranean experience had led

6th March. While Freyberg waited for the rain and snow to end before beginning the next round, American mortars continued to shell Cassino

When the rain stopped on the 7th, the landscape was 'indistinguishable from the Somme or Passchendaele'

Above: First aid men pick up the wounded on a road near the town. *Below:* An American 155mm gun in action against German mortars

him to expose some of the inadequacies in the OVERLORD plan which he and Montgomery inherited when they reached Britain. It was clear to both men that more divisions were required in the assault phase of OVERLORD and hence more shipping. Assuming that the shipping could not be found from new production or from the Pacific, it could come only from ANVIL under existing plans. Eisenhower was unwilling to allow even ANVIL to take resources which he found that he needed for OVERLORD.

The situation thus arose in which the British were arguing with Eisenhower that the best Mediterranean operation was the one which served OVERLORD best. It was ironical that the American Chiefs of Staff found themselves standing by ANVIL which did not serve the best interests of OVERLORD.

A temporary compromise was reached. Eisenhower proposed that Italian operations should have priority over all others in the Mediterranean provided the Supreme Command Mediterranean continued to make plans and preparations for a seaborne diversion to help OVERLORD. The existing fleet of assault shipping was to stay in the Mediterranean until 20th March when there would be a review of its future. If it were then decided that a major amphibious assault to assist OVERLORD could not be mounted, all but that required for a cover plan operation would return to Britain.

These proposals were accepted by the President and the Prime Minister on 26th February. On the 28th, Alexander discussed his new plans for DIADEM with the army commanders at Caserta.

Associated with the new look of the strategy in Italy there had to be wholesale regrouping of formations to prepare for the spring. Eighth Army's boundary would extend southward to include Cassino. The formations would then be divided between the two armies more rationally. Those using mainly British equipment and organisation were to be under Eighth Army command. The Fifth Army would include the French, the Americans and all the divisions in VI Corps.

The moves to implement the regrouping would take until 15th April, after which DIADEM, the battle to destroy the German armies south of Rome, could begin. But first the New Zealand Corps would attack again at Cassino to seize the bridgehead required for the spring offensive. But the new, limited role of DICKENS was not clearly reflected in the plan or the conduct of the operation which was originally intended to begin a week after AVENGER had ended.

On the afternoon of 18th February, when the survivors of A and B companies of 28th Battalion were staggering back from the station, Freyberg began planning the next round. It was not a stimulating exercise. Every variation seemed to have been played; wide flanking attacks to start with, then shorter movements. The Americans had also attacked the town from the north and their 133rd Infantry was still holed out in the houses along the Caruso Road on the edge of the town. To repeat any of these operations seemed to be futile. Yet no new surprise to spring on the defenders suggested itself.

The plan for Operation DICKENS therefore depended on dropping a stupifying weight of bombs on the defenders of the town and a rapid advance from the north by the Indians while the New Zealanders attacked up Route 6 with tank support. The new element in the plan was the use of strategic bombers. The hour of the attack was to be tied to their availability. To make certain that the ground was dry when the attack started, Freyberg decided that the bombing should take place only when three successive days without rain had been forecast.

Freyberg visited Mark Clark to discuss his plan on the evening of the 18th. Clark's first comment was that

Freyberg had left the Monastery out of account. He did not think that Cassino could be taken unless the hill were first secured, whereas Freyberg intended to take the hill from the town in the second phase. The British 78th Infantry Division, which had moved into the line south of the town, together with CCB of 1st US Armored Division would exploit up the valley while the second phase proceeded. Finally the New Zealanders would clear the banks of the Rapido from the north. Clark 'was really shocked' at the plan and drew an analogy with Sant' Angelo where he attributed the result to the failure to secure the flanks.

Freyberg no longer believed that operations against the back of the Monastery could succeed. The problems of logistics were insuperable, and while the terrain prevented the Indians from attacking on a broad front they would be slaughtered if they attacked on a narrow one. Nevertheless, Freyberg listened to Clark's criticism and altered his plan. The result was a compromise. He would now commit the Indians on a line running down the hillside from about Point 445, behind the Monastery on the right, through Point 236 above the top bend of the road, to Castle Hill on the left. The 2nd New Zealand Division would thrust into the town from the north at the foot of the hill.

Freyberg's bombing plan brought a warning from Colonel Stephen Mack of the XII Air Support Command, that although the bombers could destroy the town in about three hours, the infantry 'could advance [only] with difficulty' after the bombardment and that it would be impossible 'to get tanks through the town for two days' because the streets would be blocked with debris. According to an officer who was present, General Freyberg 'brushed aside' Mack's statement. If it proved that our side could not use tanks, neither could the enemy, he declared. Nevertheless, he expected his tanks to be through the town in six to twelve hours.

There existed a body of filed information about the effect of heavy aerial bombardment in the battle zone. For instance, there were reports on German bombing at Stalingrad and on British experience at Battipaglia in the Salerno bridgehead. This information was not made available to the New Zealanders. However, it should be noted that opinion on the subject remained divided despite the disappointing results which were to be obtained at Cassino. Above all, it must be recorded that the bombardment was undertaken as an experiment which would cost materials rather than lives. All could agree on this approach for everything else had been tried.

A number of preliminary moves were required before 24th February which was the earliest date on which DICKENS could start. The 5th Brigade of 4th Indian Division had to be brought down the hill so that it could attack on the right of the New Zealanders. It was to be relieved on the night of 23rd February in its positions opposite the Point 450-445 ridge by battalions of 11th Brigade. All troops behind the Monastery would then be commanded by 7th Brigade. The Americans of 36th Division, still on Monte Castellone, would be relieved by the French. The 133rd Infantry was relieved by 6th New Zealand Brigade in the northern outskirts of the town on the night of 21st February. The 6th Brigade was to assault.

Heavy snow on the 23rd delayed the reliefs in the mountains and 5th Indian Brigade was not back in Caira village, their base for DICKENS, until the 25th. Their attempt to secure Point 445, the right and upper end of the start line for the sweep across the east face of Monastery Hill, had failed on the night of 22nd February.

The positions taken over by 6th Brigade formed a narrow wedge at the base of the mountains along Caruso Road. On the right was Point 175 facing the Castle which was still held by the Germans across a ravine. On the left, the front ran away north-eastwards along Pasquale Road. In the middle, at the point of the wedge, they held houses round the junction of these two roads and another, called Parallel Road, which ran between them.

The snow and rain which started to fall on the 23rd continued day after day until 7th March. Although fine days followed, and the tracks became fit for the armour again, the Foggia airfields were so saturated that the bombers could not take off. But at last, on 15th March, the bombers were ready and the operation could start.

The delay had not improved the corps' chances of success. *Taihoa* had blunted its spirit a little and the sickness rate, a good barometer of morale, had risen. Security was imperilled because it was common knowledge that the town was to be bombed. Everyone had looked forward to the spectacle in February, but by mid-March the show had been running too long. Then on 2nd March, General Kippenberger, not only the divisional commander but a much loved character, was severely wounded in a minefield on Monte Trocchio.

At least the gunners, who never rested even when the units which they supported did, used the interval to good effect. Their observation officers stared out on the desolate scene, day after day, and leaped to phone and radio at the appearance of even a single German minding his own business in a back area. When the rare target of importance appeared, hundreds of shells converged upon it. The landscape was soon indistinguishable from the Somme or Passschendaele. The area from which the 71st Nebelwerfer Regiment fired its hated rockets was like a ploughed field with shell holes almost lip to lip. Most feared by the Germans were the air observation planes which fluttered over the river line and pounced on any German gun which dared to fire. The choice of gun positions was so limited that it was difficult to escape their notice. British gunners, who remembered the siege of Tobruk in 1941 and the Fieseler Storch called 'The Baron' which used to make their lives a misery, were glad that the tables had been turned.

Behind the Monastery, the 7th Brigade was losing about sixty men a day from a steady shower of rifle grenades and mortar bombs, the shelling of the reverse slopes and from exposure. Short rounds, usually tactfully attributed to guns from other divisions or corps, continued to land in the battalion areas. Both sides conducted a propaganda campaign by pamphlets fired behind enemy lines by artillery which recorded the most depressing items of news. The German messages were written in Urdu as well as English.

The isolation of the brigades behind the Monastery was reduced by improvements to the track called Cavendish Road leading up from Caira village. New Zealand compressors and bulldozers and Indian engineers and pioneers widened the road until it was fit for tanks as far as Madras Circus. During Operation DICKENS a force of tanks was to thrust up the valley between Monte Castellone and Snakeshead and surprise the defenders of Albaneta. They would then exploit along the track under Point 593 and rush the Monastery from the rear.

The interval between AVENGER and DICKENS had been used to good effect by XIV Panzer Corps to settle 1st Parachute Division firmly in the Cassino sector, to pull out some of the mobile units and to concentrate scattered divisions.

Baade had persuaded Vietinghoff that as the destruction of two battalions of 29th Panzer Grenadiers at Anzio had required 15th Panzer Grenadier Division to send 1st and 2nd 129th Panzer Grenadiers as a replacement, and the resulting hole had had to be plugged by 2nd/361st

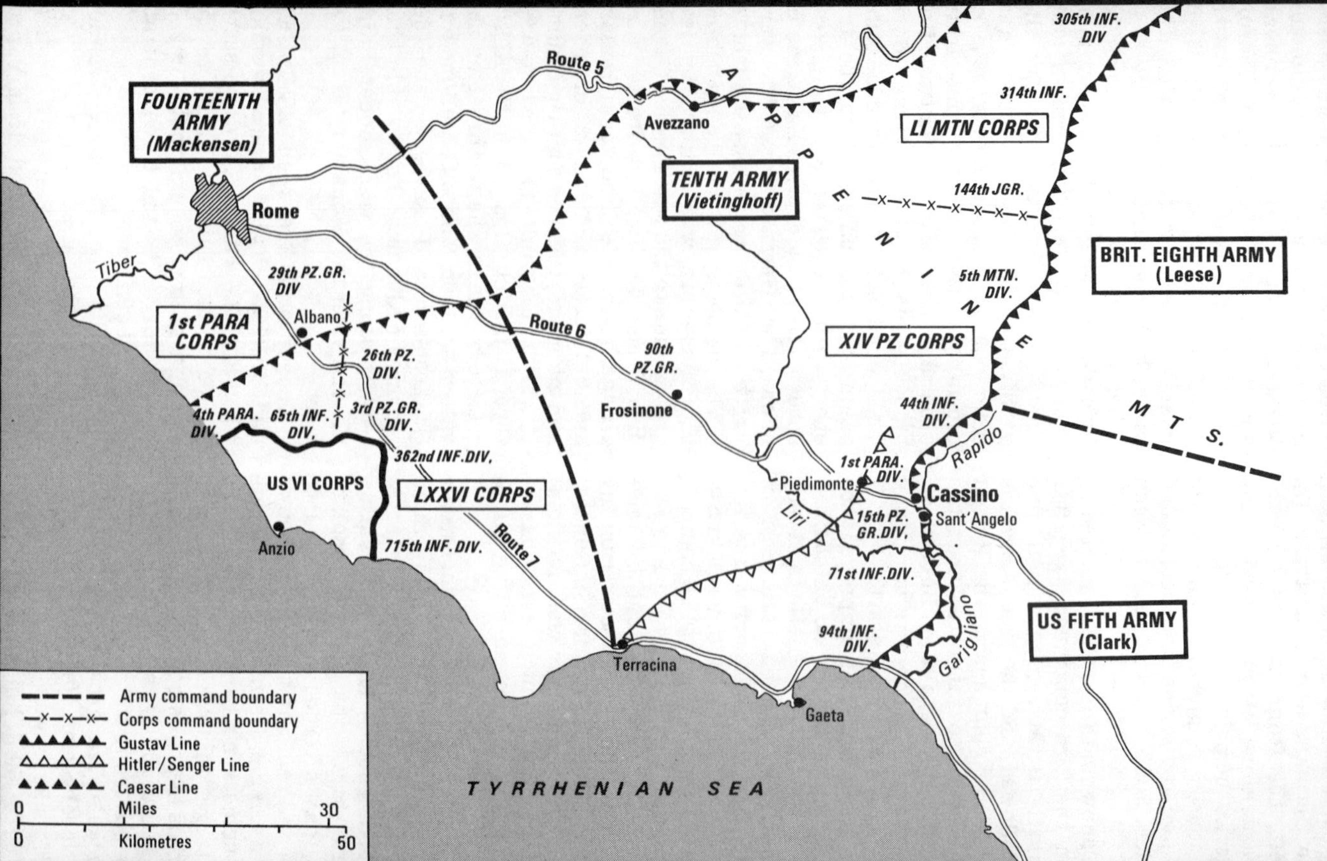

Approximate disposition of German forces at the beginning of March

Panzer Grenadiers and 44th Division's reconnaissance battalion, his division ought not to be sent north to the Adriatic as had been planned. Consequently, 51st Mountain Corps, which was now responsible for the Adriatic sector, was left with only 334th and 305th Infantry Divisions plus a reinforced regimental group, and 90th Panzer Grenadiers went into reserve behind XIV Corps. The 44th Division, the units of which had been pulled out of the line in rotation, now replaced the mobile units of the 90th and 3rd Panzer Grenadiers in the line and allowed 191st Grenadier Regiment to join the rest of 71st Infantry between 15th Panzer Grenadier Division and 94th Infantry. The Parachutists had already relieved the illustrious 211th Grenadiers of that division in Cassino town. The 1st Parachute Regiment was in the northern sector opposite the French with IV Alpine Battalion in support on Monte Caira; 4th Parachute Regiment was in the Albaneta-Colle Sant' Angelo area, and the 3rd Regiment had 2nd Battalion in the town and the others near Montecassino itself. The Parachute Machine Gun Battalion was in the south end of the town. The division was below strength. None of its battalions had more than 360 men, and the average was only 200.

Heidrich had been more fortunate than his predecessor in being given time to organise the defence. As the forward positions were under fire much of the time it had not been possible to provide the men with underground shelters. But in a second line, immediately in the rear, good progress was made in shoring up caves and strengthening cellars with concrete. Supplies were stockpiled in the town and in Montecassino. It was assumed that the Via Casilina would no longer be usable during the coming battle and that supplies would have to be run into the town from the mountain and vice versa. As supply parties had suffered many casualties, alternative routes were found avoiding areas which Allied artillery harassed systematically. To prevent the New Zealanders penetrating the southern outskirts of the town Heidrich established a switch line in the area of the Baron's Palace and the Roman Theatre. Medium machine guns and anti-tank guns were located there to prevent a thrust from the area of the station or the exploitation of a breakthrough in the town.

Senger placed Cassino second to the 94th Division front on his list of danger spots. There, *Osttruppen* still held the coastal defences between Gaeta and Terracina and he was afraid of landings behind the front.

As usual, Tenth Army had difficulty in determining what Fifth Army intended. Wentzell had to make a search of prisoners' documents in the hospitals. For not one prisoner had been brought in from Cassino, which was 'enough to drive one round the bend.' The composition of the Polish Corps was a mystery until 12th March. Intelligence could not discover the whereabouts of II US Corps, and on 13th March it was still believed that the New Zealanders had been withdrawn from Cassino. An attack by 15th Panzer Grenadiers on 19th February, part of Kesselring's orders to keep Fifteenth Army Group in a state of unrest and to take prisoners, cost it over one hundred casualties, including thirty-five prisoners. Prisoners from the new US 88th Infantry Division had been taken near Minturno on 8th March but they were so stubbornly reticent that it was not until the 16th that their captors could confirm it.

When the Fifth Army had still made no move on 11th March, Kesselring decided to go on leave. Although his field officers were becoming steadily more bemused by the uncertainty which shrouded Allied dispositions on the southern front, he believed that nothing 'big' was intended until the spring weather started.

Operation Dickens

The final plan for DICKENS, which began on 15th March, was almost the same as the original one written on 21st February. The troops would withdraw before dawn to a safety line 1,000 yards from Cassino and the bombing would last from 0830 hours until 1200 hours. Five hundred aircraft, medium bombers beginning and ending the performance, would drop 1,000 tons of bombs on an area measuring 1,400 yards by 400. In the afternoon fighter-bombers would be on call to attack prearranged targets.

H-hour for the New Zealanders was midday. A barrage, lifting one hundred yards every six minutes, would lead A and B Companies of the 25th Battalion of 6th Brigade through the northern part of the town to the line of Route 6. On the right, D Company would advance from Point 175 to seize Castle Hill as a jumping off point for 5th Indian Brigade's operation on the hillside above the town. The tanks of 19th Armoured Regiment would give close support to 25th Battalion; 5th New Zealand Brigade and CCB of 1st Armoured Division would fire into the town from the left

0830 hours, 15th March. The massive Allied airstrike against Cassino begins

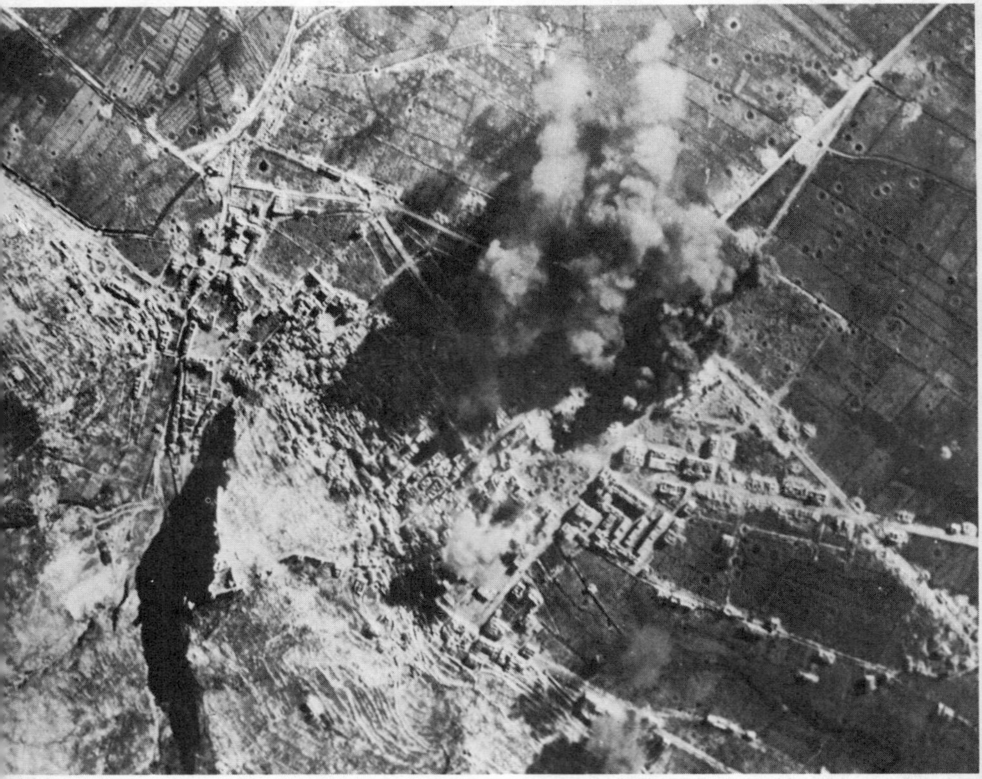

500 aircraft dropped 1,000 tons of bombs on an area 1,400 yards by 400.

flank. The first phase, objective 'Quisling', was to be completed by 1400 hours. By that time the Essex Regiment of 5th Indian Brigade would relieve D Company on Castle Hill.

In the second phase, objective 'Jockey', 6th Brigade would continue southward to the Baron's Palace where Route 6 turns west round the foot of Monastery Hill. On the left they would take the station and the area of the hillock and then advance astride the Gari and its tributaries. Meanwhile, 5th Indian Brigade would advance across and up the face of Monastery Hill to capture Point 435, called Hangman's Hill. The 7th Indian Brigade would demonstrate against the north side of the Monastery and take advantage of any German weakness.

During the night of 15th March, New Zealand and American engineers would bridge the river on both the railway and the Route 6 entries to the town from the east. The 5th New Zealand Brigade would take over the station area and the tanks of CCB and the rest of the New Zealand armour would move into the bridgehead ready to exploit.

By the end of the first night the Indians should have seized the Monastery, but whether or not they had done so the exploitation phase into the Liri valley would begin at first light.

Despite the new emphasis at Alexander's headquarters on DIADEM which had resulted from Harding's appreciation at the end of February, the exploitation phase of DICKENS was similar to that of AVENGER. However, a new development was that 78th Infantry Division would cross

Light anti-aircraft gun

the Rapido at Sant' Angelo on the night of 16th March to broaden the bridgehead to include some of the hills on the south side of the Liri valley and to cause the Germans to disperse their artillery effort. Another addition concerned a tank force which was to use Cavendish Road. A mixed force of American and New Zealand armour under the 7th Indian Brigade Reconnaissance Squadron was to advance from Madras Circus at first light on the 16th and arrive at the west side of the Monastery in time to support 5th Indian Brigade's assault from the east.

The artillery fire plan was on an enormous scale. A variety of unusual participants, including three Italian-manned railway guns and a few others which were supernumerary and were generally referred to as 'Bush Arty', brought the numbers which played a part in the battle to about 900. The programme called for 1,200 tons of high explosive to be fired at the objectives and known hostile batteries in four hours.

Although four or five tons of explosive had been allowed for every German defender, it was realised that that did not ensure success. While the defenders in the northern part of the town might succumb, those further back had better shelters and might recover before the infantry were upon them. There was also a danger that when the advanced sub-units withdrew beyond the bombline, the defenders would infiltrate forward into their vacant positions. The narrow front of the advance, which was overlooked from the hillside, prevented rapid and simultaneous engagement of the defenders who might have time to seal off the penetration. Finally

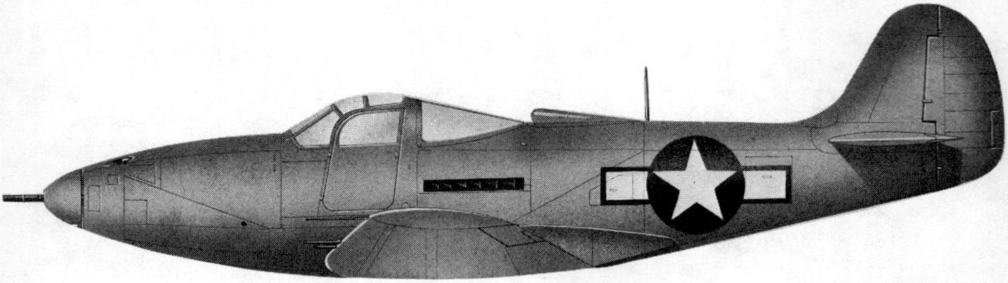

The North American B-25 Mitchell was numerically the most important American bomber of the Second World War. It was an easy aeroplane to fly, had a good performance and proved capable of accepting the ever increasingly heavy armament and armour required by combat conditions. Illustrated is a B-25C. *Engines:* two Wright R-2600 radials, 1,700hp at take off. *Armament:* six .5-inch Browning machine guns with 2,100 rounds of ammunition and up to 3,000lbs of bombs. *Speed:* 284mph at 15,000 feet. *Climb:* 16½ minutes to 15,000 feet. *Ceiling:* 21,000 feet. *Range:* 1,500 miles with 3,000lbs of bombs, 2,750 miles maximum. *Weight empty/loaded:* 20,300/35,000lbs. *Span:* 67 feet 7 inches. *Length:* 52 feet 11 inches

The Bell P-39 Airacobra was designed as an interceptor, but proved most successful in the ground attack and fighter-bomber roles. In an effort to give their new fighter maximum manoeuvrability, the Bell design team placed the engine in the middle of the aircraft, behind the pilot, with the propeller being driven by means of a ten foot extension shaft from the engine. The idea was that placing the engine on or near the centre of gravity would reduce the moments of inertia and thereby bestow great agility on the machine, besides giving the designers the opportunity to add a tricycle undercarriage, with its better landing characteristics, a heavier nose mounted armament and better visibility for the pilot. The prototype proved dissapointing as an interceptor as a result of its considerable weight and poor engine, but its armour sturdiness and armament made it a formidable low level army support weapon, and it was in this field that the P-39 made its mark. *Engine:* Allison V-1710 liquid-cooled inline engine, 1,325hp. *Armament:* one M4 37mm cannon with 30 rounds, four .5-inch Browning machine guns, two with 200 and two with 300 rounds per gun and one 250, 325 or 500lb bomb. *Speed:* 376mph at 15,000 feet. *Climb:* 4 minutes to 10,000 feet. *Ceiling:* 35,000 feet. *Range:* 525 miles at 10,000 feet at 250mph (clean). *Weight empty/loaded:* 5,645/8,300lbs. *Span:* 34 feet. *Length:* 30 feet 2 inches

One of the Second World War's greatest aircraft, the North American P-51 Mustang was used in nearly every theatre of the war. The original version was handicapped by possessing an Allison engine whose power dropped off very markedly at altitude, and a cockpit canopy which gave the pilot a view which before the war would have seemed adequate, but which war experience had proved to be at a disadvantage in combat. The installation of the Packard-built Rolls-Royce Merlin solved the first problem, and the Malcolm hood and finally the cut-down bubble canopy the second. Both these features were embodied in the P-51D illustrated, the D being the first version to have both advantages. The Mustang was almost viceless, and had great manoeuvrability at all altitudes, a very good turn of speed, the ability to fly long ranges, considerable firepower and bombload and extreme strength and robustness. *Role:* single seater interceptor, long-range escort fighter and fighter-bomber. *Engine:* one Packard V-1650 Merlin 12-cylinder inline, 1,695hp at 6,000 feet. *Armament:* six .5-inch Browning machine guns with 400 rounds per gun (inner pair) and 270 rounds per gun (centre and outer pairs) (illustrated), or four .5-inch Browning machine guns with 400 rounds per gun, and two 500lb or 1,000lb bombs or six 5-inch rockets. *Speed:* 437mph at 25,000 feet. *Climb:* 7.3 minutes to 20,000 feet. *Ceiling:* 41,900 feet. *Range:* 950 miles clean at 395mph at 25,000 feet or 1,300 miles at 260mph at 10,000 feet or 2,080 miles at 244mph at 10,000 miles with two 91.6 gallon drop tanks. *Weight empty/loaded:* 7,125/12,100 lbs. *Span:* 37 feet 0¼ inch. *Length:* 32 feet 3 inches

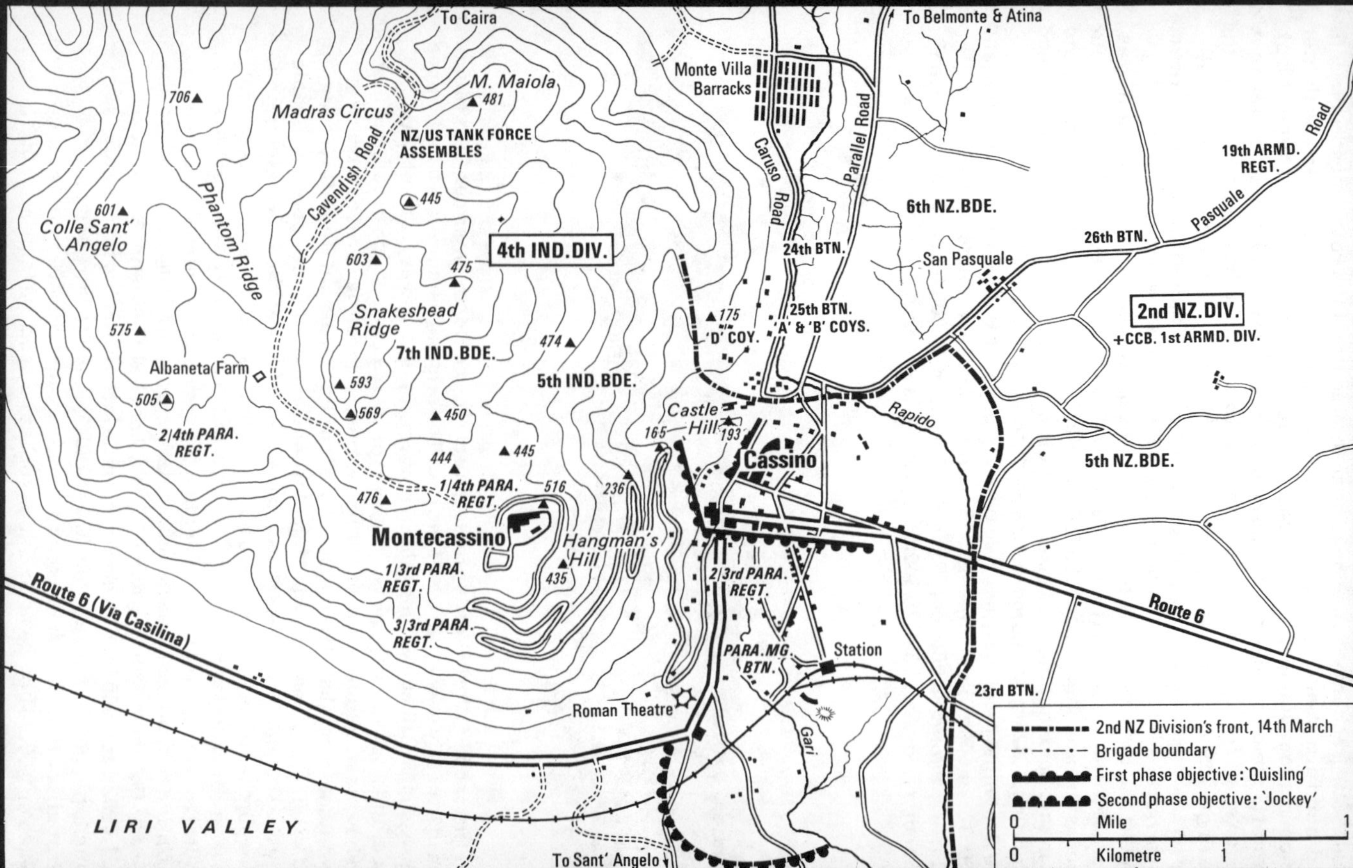

Disposition of 4th Indian and 2nd New Zealand Divisions and objectives for Operation Dickens

the bombing might destroy all landmarks, and the rubble make the town impassable to tanks while it provided the surviving defenders with a continuous belt of concealed fire positions.

The bombardment was watched from Cervaro by Freyberg, Alexander, Clark and Lieutenant-General Ira Eaker, Tedder's successor as Allied Air Commander in the Mediterranean. Tight formations of medium bombers were followed by more ragged ones of heavies. Half of the bombs landed on the target; most of the others fell outside because the dust and smoke obliterated the target from the sight of bomb aimers. Those which fell as far away as Allied gun areas, transport lines and even on a hospital were less excusable. One complete group of heavies bombed Venafro which was over ten miles from Cassino. One hundred and forty civilians were killed or wounded. In terms of casualties the Germans suffered less than the Allies and civilians.

As the last mediums droned away, Cassino was entirely laid waste. Not a building remained intact. Here and there a ruin remained unsteadily erect above what was now a single heap of rubble. When the guns opened up many of them subsided too.

The two companies of 25th Battalion followed the barrage in along Caruso Road with B Squadron of 19th Armoured Regiment behind them. They passed their old positions and then the road running past the jail. A few hundred yards beyond they met resistance. There was brisk fire from Castle Hill on the right flank. Machine guns and snipers fired unexpectedly from the ruins of the buildings which they had entered and forced them into small infiltrating groups. The usually unreliable radio net between companies and battalion headquarters collapsed at 1300 hours. Snipers killed the runners who carried messages and the linesmen who were laying cables behind the advance. The tanks were unable to follow the infantry who by now were clambering over piles of concrete and girders and crossing sixty-foot craters. Smoke and dust still enveloped the ruins. It was hard to maintain direction. Even the loom of the hill on the right was not an effective aid because most of the fire came from the caves and ruined buildings clinging to its side and at its foot, and the infantry tended to swing off to the left to avoid it. The leading companies became intermixed. Control was soon lost and it was difficult to maintain forward momentum. Small pockets of Germans, continually on the move from position to position in the smoke, made the clearance of the town into an unpleasant game of cops and robbers. In the afternoon, German artillery joined in the battle from the Belmonte-Atina area, where it was protected by steep hills, and *nebelwerfers* came out of hiding from beyond Villa Santa Lucia to make conditions even more unpleasant.

By 1530 hours, A Company had advanced past the Nunnery on the left and a platoon had reached the convent on Route 6. There they shared the remains of the large, sturdy building with Germans who prevented any further advance. Unsupported, the platoon had to withdraw. Another platoon turned right down the northern fork of Route 6 with the intention of getting behind the Germans who were opposing B Company. But they were halted after a hundred yards. B Company met stiffer resistance in the buildings under the hill and could not reach its first objective which was Route 6. The last line of the barrage along Route 6 was fired twice more to help the companies forward in the evening and concentrations fell on troublesome mortars in the area beyond. But the real need was for more troops properly organised and they were not forthcoming. C Company, 25th Battalion's reserve, went forward to the area of the jail and the Nunnery, not to press the attack but to maintain communications. It was midnight before B Company of 24th Battalion arrived in A Company's area as the

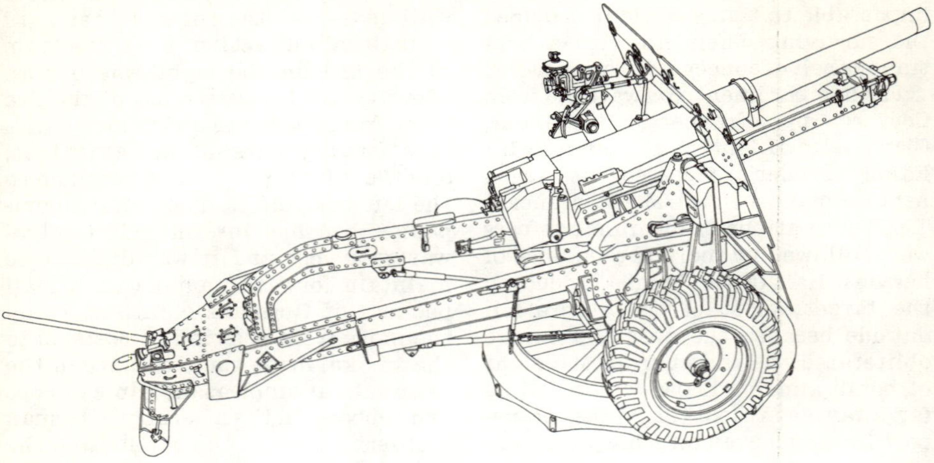

The British 25-pounder Gun Howitzer is one of the world's classic artillery pieces. It began to be issued early in the Second World War as a replacement for the earlier 18-pounder and 4.5-inch howitzer of First World War vintage. It soon became the standard weapon of the field artillery. During the course of the war, experience with the gun in the anti-tank role led to the development of a muzzle brake, which reduced recoil when the gun was firing armour piercing shells. A circular firing table was also produced to give the weapon unlimited traverse. *Weight:* 1.8 tons emplaced. *Traverse:* 350 degrees when mounted on firing platform. *Elevation:* −5 degrees to +42 degrees. *Range:* 12,500 yards (normal charge), 13,400 yards (super charge). *Rate of fire:* four rounds per minute. *Muzzle velocity:* 1,470 feet per second when firing HE shell with a normal charge. *Ammunition:* 25lb HE, 22lb smoke and 20lb AP. *Crew:* NCO and five men

only paltry reinforcement.

The tanks were prevented from entering the town by enormous craters on Parallel Road and did not find a detour round those on Caruso Road until 1300 hours. But then, rubble at the entrance to the town prevented their following B Company towards the junction with Route 6 near the Hotel Continental. A troop of another squadron came in from Pasquale Road and did better. But only after the crews had cleared the rubble themselves. The engineers declared that they could not come forward because of fire from Castle Hill. Four tanks reached the Nunnery and gave some fire support to the infantry near the convent. Another troop tried to work round by the boundary road but was held up by craters.

In street fighting, tanks were decisive but only when they worked in collusion with infantry squads. Radio communication was difficult because of obstructions and the best team work was at the lowest level when a pair of tanks covered each other while one of them fired several rounds into a building seconds before the infantry squad rushed in with grenades. Because of the rubble, the tanks seldom got close enough to the infantry at Cassino to locate them or their opponents exactly. Precision, the very essence of tank fire, could not be applied: the bludgeon of bombs and artillery shells could not be followed by the rapier of the 75mm tank gun.

The gloomy story of frustration in

the town was relieved by the exploit of D Company of the 25th Battalion at the Castle. While the battle was going on below them, a platoon approached Castle Hill from the ravine which divides it from Point 175 on the north. Climbing up the rocky wall of the ravine on all fours, they emerged in the scrub which flanked the German defence posts round Point 165. Covered by light automatics, they rushed a yellow house and took two prisoners. Then, bringing fire to bear on a nearby pillbox, they charged in again and took a company headquarters and twenty-three prisoners.

The platoon was now separated from the Castle by the drawbridge of lower, broken ground between Point 165 and the Castle on Point 193. But the fire-fight had alerted the Castle defenders who realized that they were being taken in the rear. The defenders on Point 236 above them had also woken up and the New Zealanders were forced to go to ground by fire from both sides.

The other two platoons of D Company were working their way round the foot of Castle Hill but making slower progress. By about 1500 hours they had reached only the point from which they were to start the steep ascent to the broken north-east fascia of the Castle. Scrambling up, they surprised some defenders who retired into an inner keep through an archway. In close pursuit they caught a Spandau in the courtyard on the other side which was firing out towards Point 165. After a prolonged grenade battle, the fort was in their hands with another twenty-two prisoners by 1645 hours.

At last light, 16th Platoon had to be called into the Castle from its exposed position on Point 165 as the 1st/4th Essex had not appeared to relieve the New Zealanders.

The news of D Company's success had been slow to reach battalion headquarters because the radio links had failed. Irrecoverable time was lost during which the Essex might have been pouring up the hill to relieve the New Zealanders and consolidate the corner of the hill which they had won. Consequently, the deployment of the rest of 5th Indian Brigade was delayed and an opportunity to surprise the hillside defences was lost. According to the plan, Hangman's Hill was supposed to have been in the hands of the Gurkhas by dusk.

The German accounts of AVENGER are coloured by General Heidrich's personal and proprietory attitude to the Cassino battlefield. His behaviour reflected, admirably, the cocky, gang-spirit of his men fighting in their underworld among the ruins. Heidrich was determined that no other units but his own should gain the kudos for defending the town and the hill, and that no superior commander should dictate to him how he ran the battle. To this end, his reports were vague and concealed rather than revealed the truth to his corps commander. Only after crises had been surmounted were they discovered to have existed, and when they were represented as still desperate it was usually to make his eventual success in surmounting them appear the more praiseworthy.

Senior officers had to visit Heidrich's headquarters to find out what was going on. But they noticed that he was inclined to be absent, like many wise commanders. When they had uncovered what they took to be the truth and begun to be perturbed it was usually too late, for the situation had changed.

The initial divisional report at 1300 hours on the 15th concentrated on the ferocity of the air bombardment which had fallen on 2nd/3rd Parachute in the town and partly on 1st/3rd on the hill. But as no more news came from the division until the evening, XIV Corps was left entirely in the dark about the ground fighting and the casualties from the bombing. It could only be hoped that the confidence everyone had in the parachutists was well placed. At last the evening report arrived. But it simply noted a few

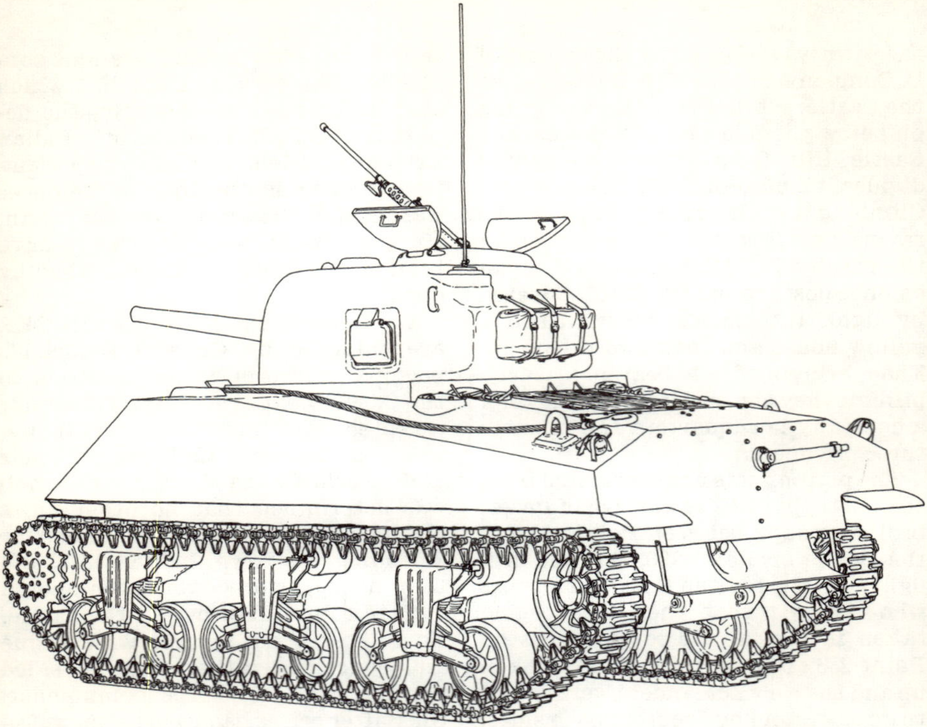

The M4A3 – E8 model of the basic Sherman medium tank was introduced in 1944. ***Crew:*** **Five.** ***Weight:*** **37.1 tons.** ***Speed:*** **26mph on roads.** ***Radius of action:*** **155 miles under optimum conditions and on roads.** ***Armament:*** **one 76mm gun with 71 rounds, one .5-inch machine gun with 600 rounds and one .3-inch machine gun with 6,250 rounds.** ***Armour:*** **Front 2 inches, sides 1.5 inches, turret front 3 inches, turret sides 2 inches and mantlet 3.5 inches.** ***Length:*** **19.3 feet.** ***Width:*** **9.8 feet.** ***Height:*** **9.9 feet**

local penetrations which had been sealed off: counteroperations were in course. The Castle was not specifically mentioned. There was no reference to casualties to men: however, the loss of heavy weapons, in particular assault guns, was reported to be complete. Later Heidrich's staff announced that the New Zealanders had attacked with 'weak forces', which they overestimated at two battalions. Everyone was surprised at the contrast between the weakness of the New Zealanders on the ground and the ponderous preliminary air effort.

Senger and Vietinghoff did not expect the division to be able to hold out if another air attack was unleashed on them. But when they were promised Luftwaffe air cover to deter further bombing, the soldiers cynically assured themselves that 'rain would be better still'. More practically, Kesselring placed at XIV Corps' disposal two battalions of 115th Panzer Grenadiers which had been earmarked for Anzio. 115th Panzer Grenadiers relieved 4th Parachute on the Colle Sant' Angelo so that it could come into the town on the night of 16th March. Heidrich believed that he had sufficient stock-piled supplies for the time being, but the roads into the town were pitted and covered with rubble and dead trees, and were continually harassed by fighter-bombers in daylight. Therefore, supplies could reach the forward areas only at night. His dumps would therefore be run down if the battle continued several days.

Darkness brought the rain the Germans needed. From 1830 hours onwards it teemed down, filling craters and obstructing the continuation of the fighting throughout the night in all kinds of ways. As so often happened, the luck turned against the side which had failed to take surprise by the ears. The reserve battalion, the 26th, received orders to advance only at 1725 hours. It ought to have been committed hard on the heels of the 25th. Only a single company of the 24th had been sent forward an hour earlier. Cheese-paring, the hallmark of AVENGER, also stamped DICKENS. A contribution to the breakdown of communications was the difficulty of finding a mere handful of men in a wilderness of broken stone and plaster. There had been nothing to prevent the Division using its numerical superiority in infantry even if it could not deploy much of its armour. But now it had forfeited surprise and would have to pay for it in blood.

After dark, 26th Battalion started to move up round the east side of the town to join 25th Battalion's A Company along the north arm of Route 6. It took the leading company over three hours to stumble and curse its way along what had once been a road to reach that far. There it stayed until first light. The company commander had brought an order for 25th Battalion to clear the area between the branches of Route 6. But

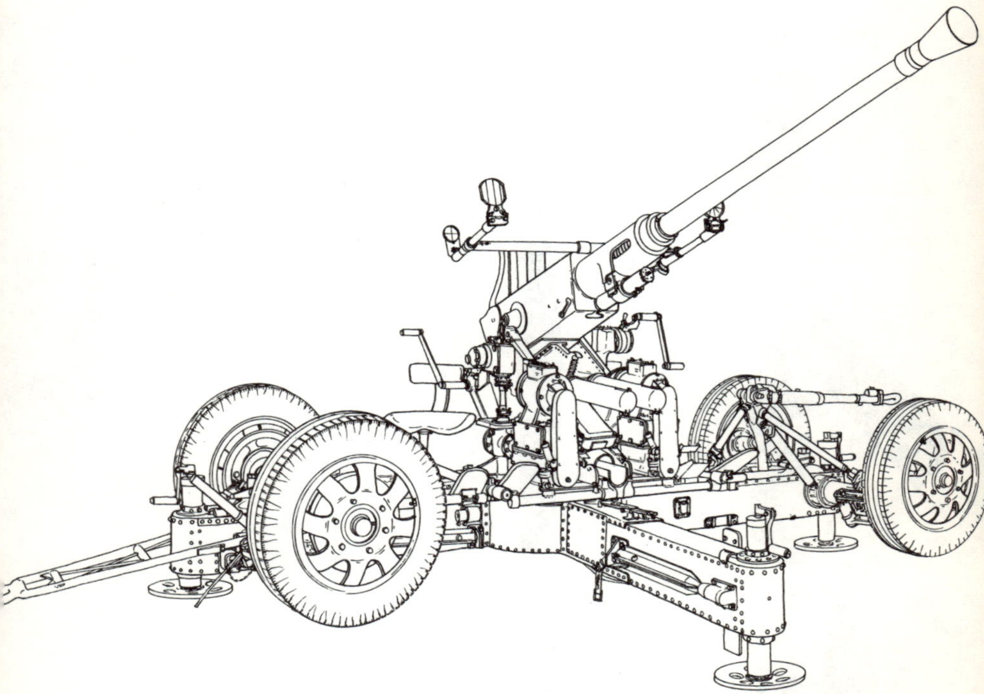

The Bofors 40mm Anti-Aircraft Gun was one of the war's most widely used weapons. Designed before the war in Sweden, it was built in great quantities in Great Britain, and was continuously updated. In action it weighed 2.4 tons, needed a crew of about six, and could fire a 2-pound shell at the rate of 120 rounds per minute to an effective altitude of 12,000 feet

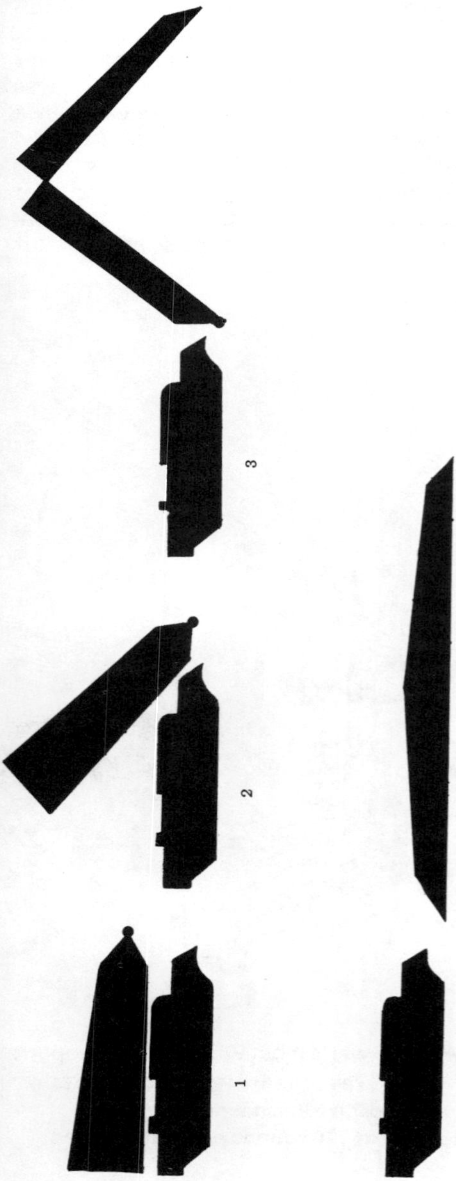
1
2
3
4

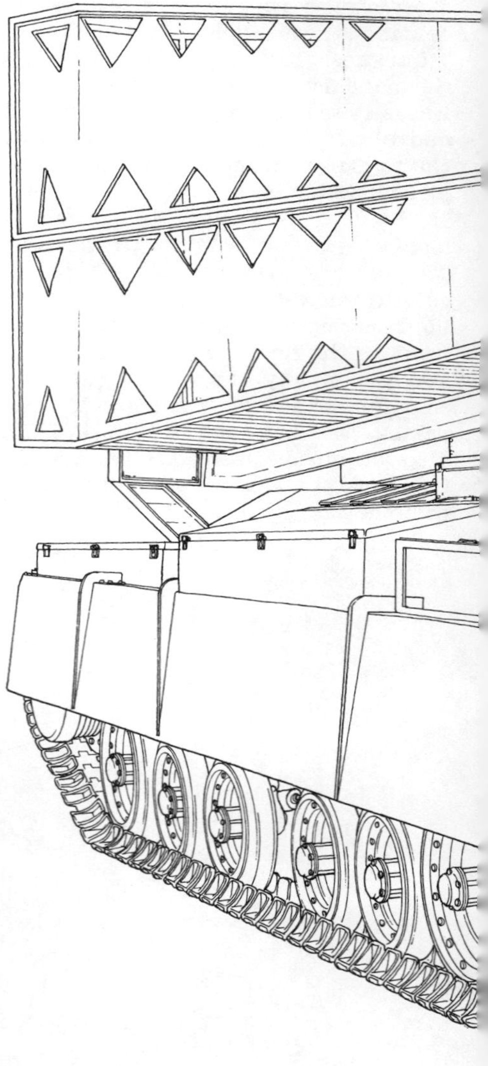

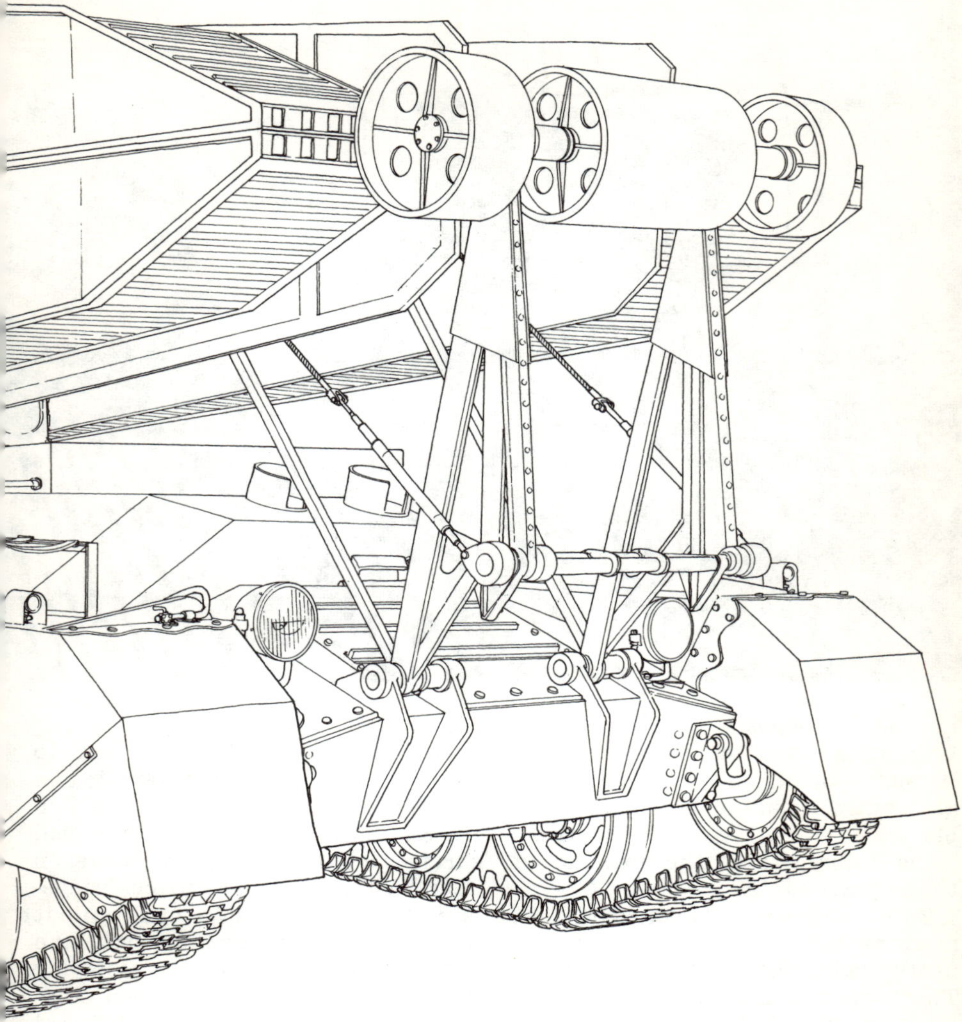

The Valentine Bridgelayer was a standard Valentine tank adapated for the bridgelaying role by the removal of the turret and the fitting of a 30 foot scissors type folding bridge. The Bridge was designed in 1936 by Lt-Col Martel and modified in its method of opening by Major Galpin of the Mechanisation Board. The bridge, as mentioned, was 30 feet long, hinged in the middle. This was carried on the tank, with the hinge at the rear. On reaching an obstacle to be bridged, the tank approached the lip of the gap, swung the front of the bridge down over the front of the tank, thus lifting the hinge up towards the vertical. As the hinge passed the vertical, the bridge began to open out, so that by the time it was horizontal the full 30 foot span had been extended, with what had been the top portion at the front of the device resting on the far lip of the gap. The bridging mechanism was known as the 'Scissors Bridge, 30 foot, No 1' and was capable of taking vehicles of up to 30 tons. Valentine bridgelayers were used in Italy, North-West Europe and Burma

he and his opposite number decided to postpone the attack until next day. It was a black and very wet night and control would have been impossible. As so often in battle, they were being ordered to do the obvious but the impracticable.

Both companies attacked next morning but after short advances to nearby ruins they were pinned down. There was no communication between them or with 25th Battalion's headquarters, and the Germans severely punished any daylight movement through the ruins. With no communications, they could not call for fire support.

Where tanks could support the infantry the results were better. One tank came down Route 6 from the east and shot a platoon of C Company of 26th Battalion back into the convent in the afternoon. This time the occupants were driven out and the position reinforced. It was the largest and most robust building remaining in the area and proved useful later as a control and staging post.

This tank was the first of several to pass over the Bailey bridge erected on Route 6 over the Rapido by the 48th US Engineer Battalion. Its crew had survived a hazardous journey to reach 26th Battalion. A Valentine bridgelaying tank was hit by a shell while it was being manoeuvred into a crater on the road. While another was replacing it, Lieutenant Morrin, a Troop Commander of A Squadron, came forward on foot and directed his tank gun at the convent with success. After another Valentine had filled the first crater, a third went forward over it to bridge the next. Only one more crater then remained. A diversion was found round that and by 1545 hours three tanks had arrived in C Company's area.

Thanks to preparatory work clearing Teller mines and filling craters by a company of the American engineers during the first night, the New Zealand engineers were able to finish the work on the next. By dawn on the 17th the tanks at the convent had a clear if shell-swept road behind them. Their radios provided invaluable communications for the infantry.

The 1st/4th Essex did not relieve D Company of 25th Battalion until midnight on the 15th. Then they learned that Point 165 had to be retaken. They were still involved in that task when the 1st/6th Rajputana Rifles started to arrive for their attack across to Point 202 and straight up the hill through Point 165 to Point 236. Unfortunately two companies of Rajputanas had been badly hit by a concentration on Caruso Road were scattered and still disorganized. Consequently only half the battalion had arrived for the assault on the hill.

Soon afterwards, the 1st/9th Gurkhas arrived below the Castle.

Left: **Among the 900 Allied guns were three Italian-manned railway guns.** ***Below:*** **1,200 tons of high explosive were fired in four hours**

Lieutenant-Colonel Nangle had heard of the fate of the Rajputanas and anticipated that he would not be able to advance to Hangman's Hill and the Monastery through firmly-held intermediate objectives. Relying on the uncanny ability of his men to move quietly at night and to keep their sense of direction, he decided to direct C and D Companies straight on to Hangman's Hill. The remainder he ordered to dig in behind the Castle where they might survive when daylight came.

C and D Companies chose what they hoped was an alternative route to the Castle because the regular route was being heavily mortared. Soon the track divided and one company took the right and the other the left fork. D Company on the right was ambushed and it was light before it could be reorganised. But C Company moved on soundlessly into the night across the hillside.

Meanwhile the two companies of 1st/

6th Rajputanas had had an unhappy time. Neither one had got within grenade-throwing range of its objective. Both came back, one to the Castle and the other to Point 165. In the morning, under cover of smoke, they attacked together up the steep and broken hillside towards Point 236. Again they failed, and a lucky mortar bomb hit their battalion headquarters, causing five officer casualties, including the commanding officer and adjutant.

Early in the afternoon of the 16th, New Zealand gunners reported that they could see figures moving about on the rocky knob of Hangman's Hill. Shortly afterwards a faint voice over the radio announced that it was C Company calling. The Gurkhas had threaded their way across the hillside and had assaulted and captured the hill. Now they were in residence. From their pinnacle they had a grandstand view of the lower slopes and the town; in turn they were overlooked from the Monastery ruins only 300 yards behind them.

The question was how to enable the rest of 1st/9th Gurkhas to infiltrate to Hangman's Hill during the coming night. Obviously the Germans on Points 202 and 236 which lay on either flank of the direct route would be alert to prevent them. So the Rajputanas attacked Point 202 with two companies and occupied it while the Gurkhas were threading their way up to Hangman's Hill. It took them eight hours. But they arrived just at the right moment. C Company was under heavy attack and the parachutists had got among the rocks of the crag. The Company Commander, Captain Drinkhall, his back against a rock and his leg broken, was urging his men to hold on. When the fresh companies arrived, the Germans prudently with-

Below: **Heidrich's paratroopers in the ruins of the Monastery** ***Right:*** **Under a Red Cross flag, British wounded move back**

drew. Drinkhall stayed in command of his company until the next day, earning the DSO for his leadership and his bravery.

Meanwhile, the other two companies of the 1st/6th Rajputanas had attacked up the hill from Point 165, yet again. This time they got to the top bend of the road below the corner of the Monastery and just under Point 236. But they were short of men and ammunition and when the parachutists launched a counterattack down the hill at the run, behind a shower of grenades, the survivors were driven off. Rather than be exposed on the hillside in daylight, they withdrew to Point 165.

By the morning of the 17th the strengths, weaknesses and possibilities of the positions of both sides had emerged. The fighting on the night of the 16th on the hill underlined them. The Germans' strength lay in the buildings tucked under the hill – particularly those near the Continental Hotel – between the two arms of Route 6, and in the caves and ruins below the Castle. Because of their sheltered position, the buildings close to the hill had not suffered so heavily as those nearer the river. Germans could infiltrate into them along Route 6 from the Baron's Palace area, and by coming down the gully from Point 445 behind the Monastery, and then creeping round the hill under the Castle.

On the hill, the Germans could reinforce Point 236 from behind the Monastery and from the Monastery ruins without difficulty. Point 236 provided the Germans with an important fire base from which they could cover the whole hillside. It could be attacked only by climbing up from Point 165 or from the gully. Even if the Indians took it, they could not hold it unless they thrust on beyond it to the Monastery itself. Hence, the best that could be done was to keep it under fire and smoke, although smoking steep hillsides was technically difficult. Yet the post remained a threat to the Indian bridgehead at the Castle.

The main weakness in the German position was its open eastern and southern flank. A New Zealand thrust towards the station and across the Gari to the Baron's Palace area might cut off the men in the town. This had been the aim of AVENGER and was to be the object of the second phase of DICKENS. If the station were firmly held by the New Zealanders, they could clear the railway causeway and bring more tanks into the battle from the east. At the same time, an operation against the houses under the hill might be mounted by infiltrating New Zealand infantry by way of the Castle to Point 202 and from there down into the town beyond the Continental Hotel. When the gully down from Point 445 had been blocked the hill would be cut off from the town.

Of course, the Germans were in a position to obstruct these developments. During the 16th the parachutists had held enough of the area between the forks of Route 6 to make an advance round their flank towards the station unacceptably expensive

Cut off for seven days, New Zealanders watch the action bog down

without tank support. And tanks had arrived in small numbers in the area of the convent only late on the 16th. On the hill, the Germans made movement impossible in daylight. In the town it was the same story. Yet, if tanks were to be used, daylight fighting was essential and the parachutists could make that very expensive.

This was the situation with which commanders at all levels had to grapple during the night of the 16th. A short answer was to use the tanks which had reached the convent to shoot 26th Battalion into the station and the area of the hillock on the

Luck turned against the side which failed to take surprise by the ears

Gari just beyond it. 24th Battalion could then be brought round to exploit to the Baron's Palace. If the engineers worked successfully on Route 6 during the night more tanks might cross the river to support them. In the meantime, 25th Battalion would have to engage the attention of the defenders of the Hotel Continental area.

There were some practical difficulties to be overcome before this straightforward plan could be effected. Even the way to the station was

pitted with bomb craters, some of which could not be avoided. It was reported that although as many as nine tanks were in the various company battle areas, six were certainly incapable of forward movement and three others probably were. The engineers' services were urgently required. But the engineers could not work until the infantry had winkled out machine gunners and snipers from the debris. The infantry needed tank support to do that. This was not quite a vicious circle but breaking it required teamwork and energetic leadership. It might be a slow business unless troop officers and individual tank commanders were sharp enough to find diversions round the obstacles.

Freyberg had always been less interested in the hill than the town and believed that the Monastery would not fall until the town was occupied. Major General Galloway, now temporarily commanding 4th Indian Division, agreed with him. A daring reconnaissance of the hillside beyond Point 202 and down to the Roman Theatre by Lieutenant Angus Murray of 4th Indian Field Company and Sergeant A F Morris of the 20th Armoured Regiment had confirmed that the road was the only route for tanks from Route 6 up to the Monastery. This meant that unless the Hotel Continental-Hotel des Roses area at the bottom of it was cleared, tank support for an assault on the Monastery would have to come up Cavendish Road. Obviously, it would be difficult to coordinate their movements with the infantry coming in from Hangman's Hill.

The decision on the night of the 26th to use tanks to shoot 26th Battalion into the station was sound. But to persevere with the attempt to clear the town with only three battalions of which only a half had been heavily committed so far was probably not. Mark Clark advised pouring

24th March. The second battle finishes and the Germans still hold Montecassino

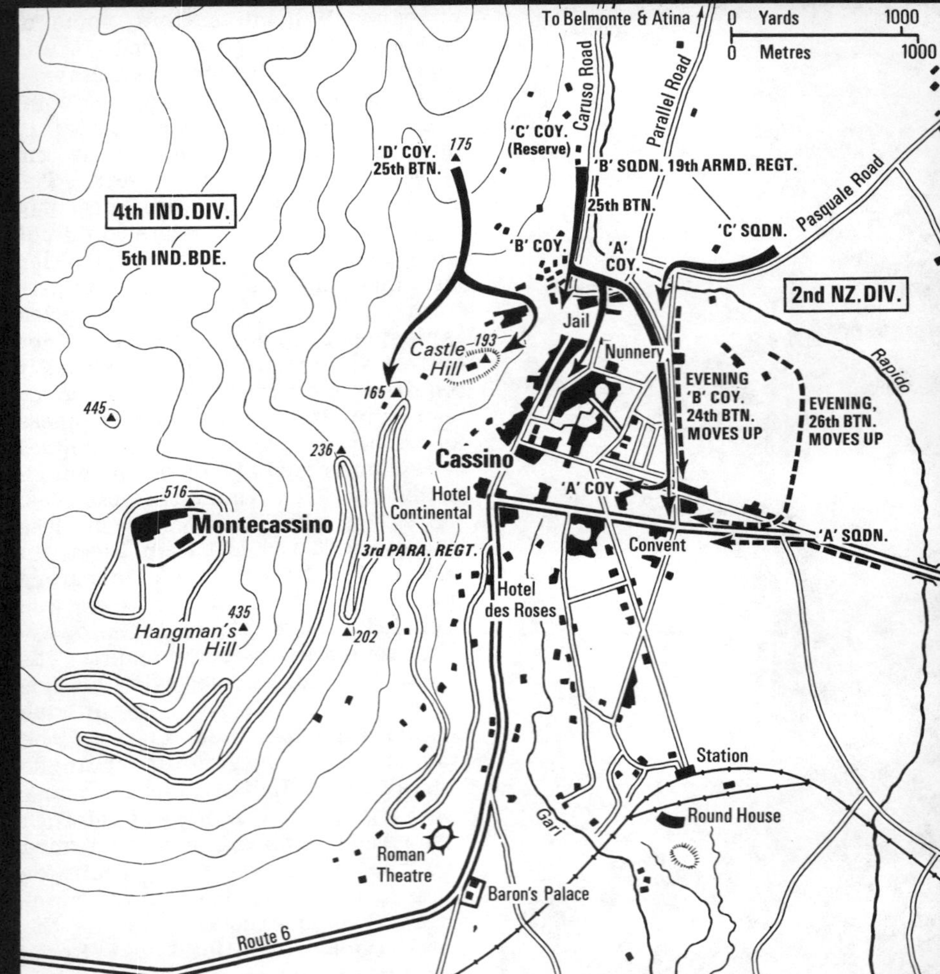

Operation Dickens: 15th March 1944, the attack begins

the infantry of 5th New Zealand Brigade or even a brigade of 78th Division over the Route 6 Bridge and into the town. Galloway agreed, remarking that he was convinced that 'the best way to clear Cassino was to put infantry in and go on doing so until it is cleared'. With the advantage of hindsight, it may seem that they were right. But Freyberg was sure that he already had plenty of infantry in the small area of the town itself, and the tanks were the answer on the outskirts. He had confidence that tanks with small squads of infantry could do the best job with fewest casualties. He must also have had one eye on the exploitation role of his division and consequently was unwilling to exhaust 5th Brigade's infantry in street fighting.

During the night of 16th March the 6th Brigade battalions in the town received hot food for the first time since the battle started. More ammunition reached them and their casualties were evacuated. When 25th Battalion and B Company of the 24th attacked towards the Hotel Continental in the morning with four tanks, they were in better heart. The direct fire of the 75mm guns of the Shermans and their 30-calibre Brownings produced good results, and in untidy house to house fighting the area between the forks of Route 6 was cleared to within 200 yards of the hotel. This provided sufficient flank protection to allow 26th Battalion to start its attack towards the station.

By 0900 hours the brigade commander, I L Bonifant, reported that he had room to work in both directions. Freyberg, having resisted outside suggestions that he commit more infantry, exhorted him to 'push on, you must go hard. Task Force B must go through as soon as possible. The limit is the roof – push hard.'

The 26th Battalion, with deficient communications and its companies scattered, arrived at the convent, which was to be on the start line, at the double and in disorder. Platoons had to run the gauntlet of snipers and machine gunners on their right flank, despite the efforts of B Company of 24th Battalion. Many men never reached the convent; others were in no state to go straight into an attack. Even C Company, which was in and around the convent already, had to be sent on its way by the CO who arrived on a tank at the last moment with the orders.

Some of A Squadron's tanks, having received orders over the radio, had gone on ahead. But the route which they had reconnoitred earlier was unrecognisable in the smoke and confusion. Consequently, the tank commanders had to lift mines and guide their tanks round obstacles on foot. Two tanks were knocked out but the crews bailed out and used their Thompsons to drive sixteen prisoners from houses in which anti-tank guns had been concealed. The other troops of A Squadron ground on towards the station. Two of them survived to support forty men of C Company as they arrived in driblets about 1300 hours. They were later joined by two tanks of another troop which had just come over the Bailey bridge on Route 6.

Major Williams sent two of his C Company platoons to occupy the round house and chase the enemy from the hillock where six prisoners were captured. From there they could observe the Baron's Palace and the Roman Theatre from which most of the enemy fire was now coming. The rest of the battalion arrived in disarray, led by junior officers, non-commissioned officers and one surviving company commander. They had followed widely different routes with varying fortunes. But when Williams and Major Harvey of B Company took stock they found that they had only about 100 men and decided to consolidate on the line of the Gari as far northwards towards the town as possible. They could not continue to the battalion objectives

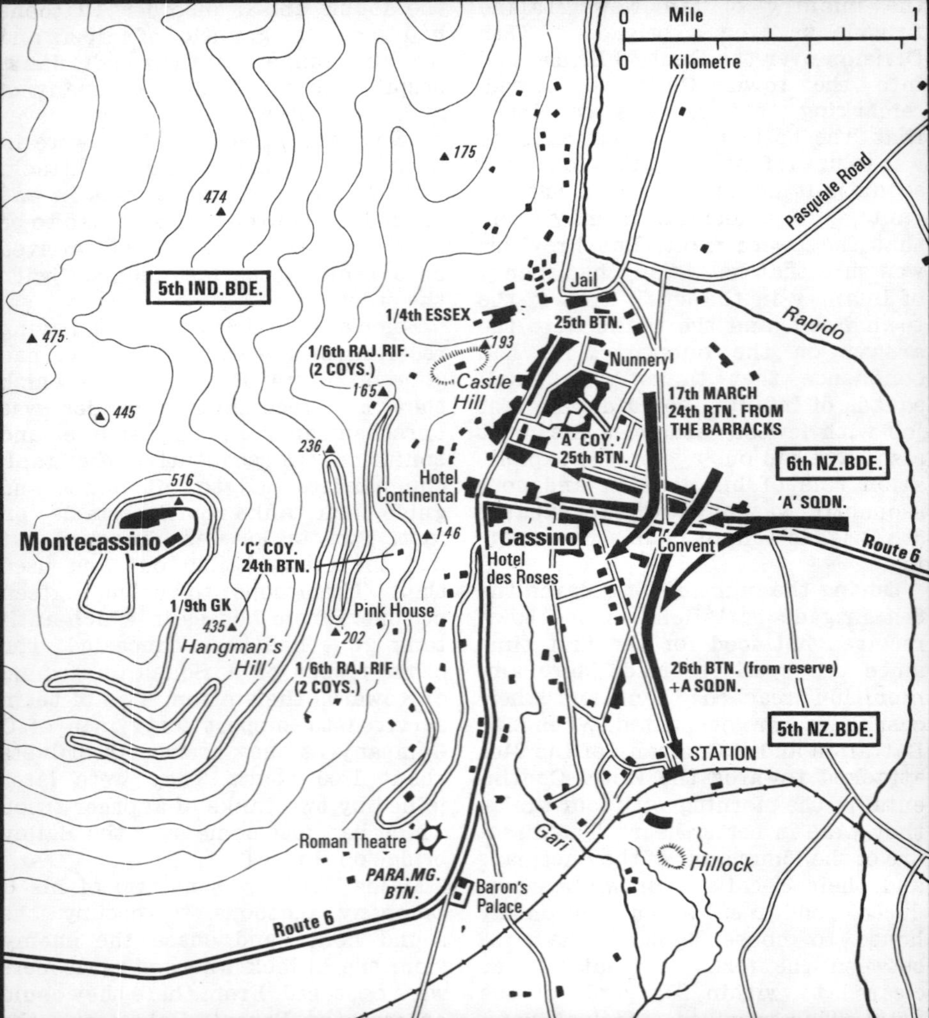

Operation Dickens: 16th/18thMarch 1944

which were the road south to Sant' Angelo and the Baron's Palace.

At that moment 24th Battalion, less B Company which was still involved in the Continental Hotel fighting, should have been passing through the station on its way to the start line for an attack from the Baron's Palace up Route 6 to the Continental Hotel. The circumstances in which 26th Battalion found itself obviously would have made this operation impossible even if 24th Battalion had arrived. But 24th Battalion had spent the night near Monte Villa barracks. Instead of being moved round by the Route 6 bridge in darkness it received no orders to move until the early afternoon. Two companies were then ordered to find their way through the town to the area south of the convent. By the time they had arrived, considerably battered by fire from positions under Castle Hill which they could not avoid, it was about 2100 hours. Then they found that their role for next day had been changed. B Company was to rejoin them and they were to fill in the gap between 25th and 26th Battalions and push forward to cut Route 6 south of the Continental.

All through the next day, the 18th, 25th Battalion continued to grind away at the wedge of Parachute-held buildings under Castle Hill and made slow and barely perceptible progress, despite some tank support. The positions of the other battalions remained much the same throughout the day. The weak 26th Battalion beat off a dawn attack by the Parachute Machine Gun Battalion across the flats from the Baron's Palace. At least ten of the sixty attackers were left as casualties.

The only new notion introduced on the 18th was to pass C Company, 24th Battalion's remaining company, through the Castle to Point 202. One platoon swept up the hillside to the 1st/9th Gurkhas while the other two went down to attack the Continental and the Hotel des Roses. The latter met intense fire from positions on the hillside and in particular from the Pink House just below Point 202. A group did reach Route 6, but Lieutenant Klaus, the 13th Platoon Commander, was killed outside the Hotel des Roses. The company then found positions round Point 146 after suffering eleven casualties. There they remained until the end of the battle.

On the 17th and 18th Heidrich brought those elements of 3rd Parachute Regiment which were still on the hill down into the town and 4th Regiment took their place. In addition, 1st Regiment began to be relieved north of Snakeshead and was fed into the town as a reinforcement. Thus, although on the 17th, 3rd Parachute was 'deemed written off' its command structure remained in existence and parachute reinforcements put a little flesh on the skeletons of its units. Under no circumstances would Heidrich allow the high standard of the defenders to be watered down by outsiders. Even the 115th Panzer Grenadiers were pronounced 'not crisis firm'. Wentzell was perfectly aware that Heidrich's reports of the operations were fanciful, but he had confidence in him and his men who were 'mad keen not to be put in the shade by Grenadier Regiment 211', the defenders of the town in February. And as long as the fighting was confined to such a small area there would be time to reinforce them from the flank if the New Zealanders looked like breaking through.

The comparatively small force which was being employed by the Allies puzzled the Germans. Kesselring feared that operations were about to begin elsewhere, while Galloway was continuing to insist that the trouble in the town was shortage of men. But General Parkinson, Kippenberger's successor, would use only 6th Brigade on the 17th and 18th although Freyberg was fast losing patience. It was obvious that the whole operation would continue to be paralysed until Cassino town was cleared up.

At last, at 1615 hours on the 18th, Parkinson decided that 28th Battalion, heroes of AVENGER, should attack through 25th Battalion at 0300 hours the next morning, to take the Continental and its associated buildings. Even then, the decision was a half-measure and was attacking the enemy at his strongest point.

The new step was to be accompanied by action on the hill. The 1st/6th Rajputanas had been amalgamated with the 4th/6th of 11th Brigade to form a full-strength battalion to garrison the Castle. The Essex would then join the Gurkhas on Hangman's Hill. The latter had received an aerial supply drop and some reserves had reached them by foot. The two battalions would assault the Monastery at dawn. The long awaited armoured thrust up the Cavendish Road to take the Monastery in the rear would coincide with this operation.

In the early morning of the 19th, C and D Companies of the Maoris, attacking with 25th Battalion on their right, made progress between the two arms of Route 6. Some men reached the bottom of the hill, but having outrun the others they had to come back. Although the tanks were unable to follow close behind the infantry, they gave effective support against riflemen and machine gunners who were firing at ground level from crevices in the tumbled concrete. But by the end of the day, although the defended area in front of the Continental was smaller and some prisoners had been taken, Hauptmann Foltin, the German Camp Commander, and his 2nd/3rd Parachute Battalion seemed as obstinate as ever. Almost all the parachutists' divisional assault guns and self-propelled antitank guns had been buried in the bombing. Since then, only two of 15th Panzer Grenadier's MK IVs' had managed to get into the town through the rubble. They had burrowed into the Continental and were giving the Maoris much trouble. But by the end of the day 19th Armoured Regiment claimed to have silenced them. After that the parachutists had to wait until the Shermans were in range of their *Faust Patronen*, an equivalent to the PIAT and Bazooka. But they were also given fire support by their artillery. *Nebelwerfers*, firing from west of the town, caused many casualties. The warhead of its rocket, if lucky enough to land inside the turret of a Sherman, had been known to turn the tank upside down. Near misses could destroy the suspension and make the tank immobile. The guns were directed by the commander of the corps artillery from Heidrich's headquarters. Oberst Heilmann, commander 3rd Parachute Regiment, also controlled a close support group of heavy mortars. Most effective was the persistent shower of 81mm mortar bombs which reached men sheltering behind walls without overhead cover. These could be fired at the rate of twenty bombs in half a minute from one tube. The crews could take cover before retaliation reached them. Their observers were in caves and ruins in the steep slopes below the Castle. Only sharp-eyed snipers and tank guns could flush them out. Snipers, quick to punish anyone who loitered in the open, were also concealed up there.

So long as Route 6 from the Baron's Palace corner to the Continental remained open, reinforcements could infiltrate into the town every night. The 6th Brigade had attempted to cut the road without success. By the 19th, most of 1st Parachute Regiment had arrived in the town by this route and 2nd/1st Parachute with 2nd/115th Panzer Grenadiers attacked 24th Battalion after dark to try to push them further from their lifeline. They attacked throughout the night but gained no ground and suffered losses. Heidrich was depressed at this failure for he had intended to follow up with an attack against the rear of 26th Battalion in the station, which was still isolated and not strong. By this means, he hoped to turn the river flank of the New Zealanders and to squeeze out the 25th and 28th Battalions.

These German attacks were to be the right claw of a counteroffensive which the successful defence of the town and the availability of 1st Parachute made possible. The left claw had already struck at 0530 hours on the 19th against 5th Indian Brigade at Castle Hill and was more effective. A Rajputana platoon had just relieved the Essex at Point 165, when about 200 men of the 1st/4th Parachute behind a brisk bombardment came down the hill at the double from Point 236 and swamped the defenders. Then they rolled on over the lower bend of the road and up to the outer walls of the Castle.

The parachutists caught 5th Brigade in the process of preparing for its attack from Hangman's Hill on the Monastery. Fortunately, they were behind schedule.

The arrangements for the night were complicated. Two companies of Rajputanas, having portered for the Gurkhas on the previous night, were to come down from Hangman's Hill. The other two companies were to relieve the Essex at the Castle and Point 165. The Essex were then to move to Hangman's Hill in two waves of two companies each. When 1st/4th Parachute attacked, two Essex companies had already left and the other two were preparing to follow them as soon as their platoon at Point 165 had been relieved. The remaining two companies of the Rajputanas were in the Castle. Tactical headquarters of 5th Brigade had also moved in because from it the Essex had been able to keep in radio communication with all brigade units. Together with a troop commander of the famous 1st Field Regiment, Royal Artillery, his crew and some sappers and miners, there were about 150 men in the Castle.

In the next few hours a medieval siege with modern weapons was fought. There were bursts of fire from loopholes on the outer wall and from the central keep. Showers of grenades were hurled over the walls in both directions and there was a steady beat of mortar bombs which seemed to fall on every inch of the ground round the Castle and on most of the courtyard within. Three times the parachutists surged down from Point 165 only to be pinned down in the broken rocks and scrub which they had to climb to reach the Castle walls. Snipers fired at the slits and at targets which appeared fleetingly in the gaps where masonry had been broken. Some riflemen from the Rajputanas went outside the walls to spot the snipers and pick off officers as they directed the assault. But the sniping continued.

By about 0830 hours the condition of the parachutists still outside the walls was worse even than that of the sixty survivors inside. Fire from Point 175 made it impossible for them to move and artillery defensive fire tasks beat the whole area between the lower bend and Point 165. An ammunition shortage inside the Castle had been partly relieved by an Essex party which brought back sandbags of ammunition and mortar bombs from Point 175 on the other side of the gully. But the mortars had fired their share of the 1,500 bombs which had fallen in the early morning and the machine gunners had used 8,000 rounds. Ammunition was not plentiful, despite the tireless work of RSM Rose.

The parachutists did not give up easily. Eight of them crept up from the town and blew down the wall on that side with a demolition charge. A swarm of men rushed through the hole and got into the courtyard. Two officers and twenty men were temporarily buried under the rubble, but a torrent of bullets from the keep swept the invaders out. Tank fire from the town pinned them down outside, although it also increased the damage to the Castle walls. While the disinterring of the defenders proceeded, a parley was held over the wall between the two sides, each trying to persuade

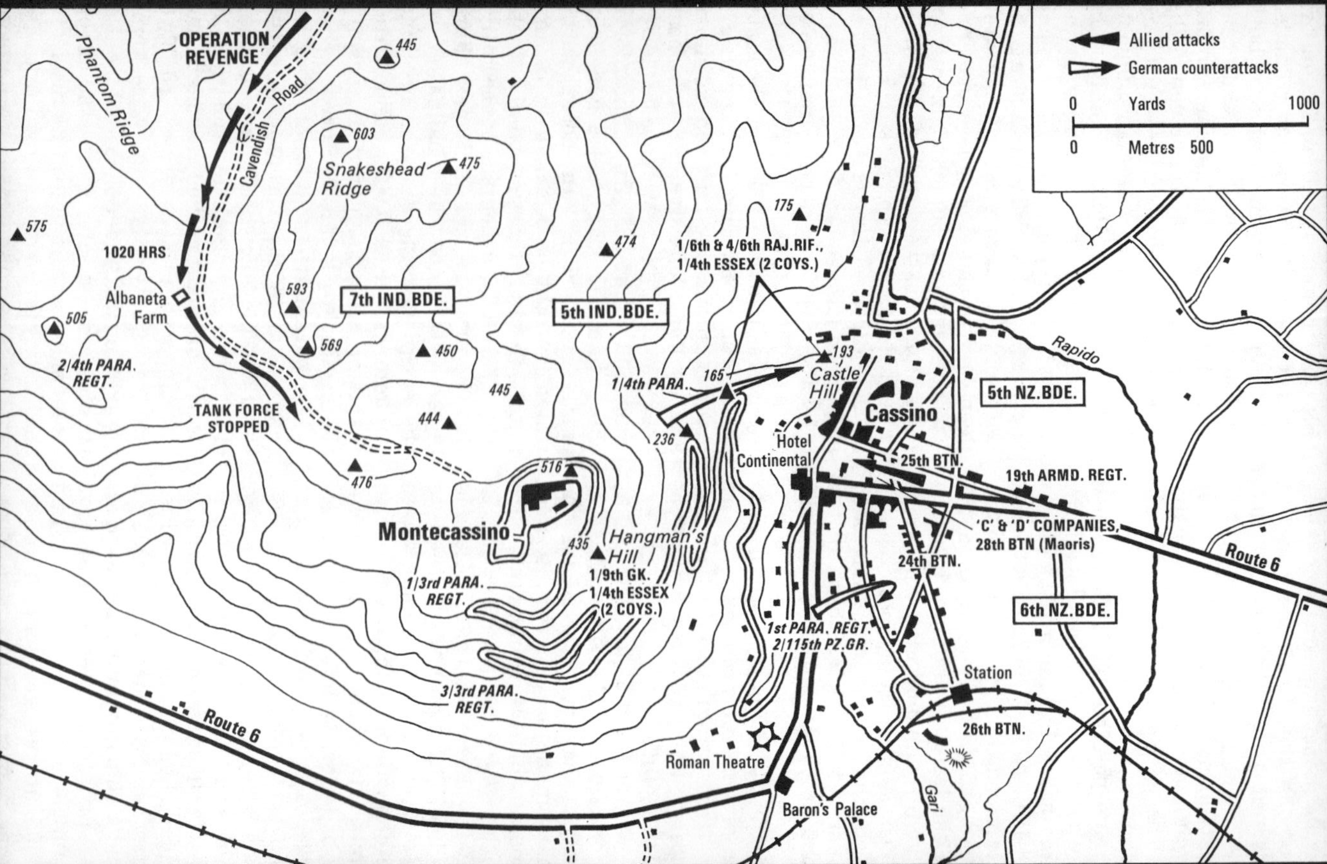

Operations Dickens (through the front door) and Revenge (through the back door) 19th March, fail

the other to surrender. By now, Major Becket was the only officer on his feet, although he had been wounded on three separate occasions. But the battle was won. The parachutists had tried everything, and their last assault was broken up by artillery fire alone.

In the meantime, the other two companies of the Essex had arrived at Hangman's Hill, except for one platoon which had been turned back and had returned to the foot of Point 175. Of those who reached the Gurkhas at 1000 hours on the 19th, only forty were able to fight and thirty were wounded. And so the attack on the Monastery which had been scheduled to start at 0600 hours had to be postponed.

The tank thrust up Cavendish Road, Operation REVENGE, had been intended to arrive at the back door of the Monastery just before the Gurkhas and the Essex arrived at the front one. It started in the hope that the infantry might yet take advantage while the attention of the defence was distracted.

The force consisted of seventeen Honey Tanks of 7th Indian Infantry Brigade's reconnaissance squadron and 760th US Tank Battalion, three 105mm SP guns of CCB 1st US Armored Division, and the Shermans of C Squadron, 20th Armoured Regiment. The whole force was commanded by a British artillery colonel without tank experience. It had no infantry with it, had not liaised closely with the 2nd Camerons of 4th Indian Division on Snakeshead, and was not familiar with the terrain, although a track reconnaissance up Death Valley had been made as far as was practicable. Finally, the men in the force were not quite sure what they were trying to do.

The column pushed up the track from the first bottleneck and over a small pass right under Point 593. At 1020 hours, much to the surprise of its German defenders, the tanks appeared before Albaneta farm and the ruined abbey and started pumping shells into both of them. Small arms and mortar fire had pursued the tanks up the valley and they had had to close down. Consequently, a number of tanks went off the narrow path and were bogged or lost their tracks. But enough of them remained to have demolished the posts round Albaneta, if they had set their minds to it.

At this stage the question arose whether they should push on up the track which ran round the back of Points 593 and 569, and then down the west side of the bowl to the Monastery, or create alarm and despondency and cause casualties in the Albaneta-Phantom Ridge area. Being in doubt, the commander called for orders by radio and had to wait in sight of the enemy until he got a reply at midday. The pause was fatal. It needed a great deal less time than that for the 2nd/4th Parachute Regiment to prepare some unpleasant surprises for the tanks.

The column was eventually ordered to advance towards the Monastery and told that if it could bring the Monastery under effective fire, the force on Hangman's Hill would attack. So the surviving Honeys lurched on past the caves under the back of Point 593 and one actually came within sight of the Monastery. But the track behind the Honeys was blocked by enterprising parachutists who placed mines on it and fired *Faust Patronen* at the tanks. It was clear that to pursue the ill-conceived scheme was going to lead to disaster. And so those tanks which could withdraw did so, hastened by everything the enemy could throw at them.

Fourteen tanks were destroyed or abandoned and the casualties to crews were significant. The Germans were warned of the possibility of tank attacks in the future and mined the approaches to Albaneta – to the disadvantage of 2nd Polish Corps when they attacked during DIADEM in May. The enterprise deserved a better fate but not enough thought had gone into its tactics. Had the operation been confined to the Phantom Ridge-Point 593-Albaneta area and been coordinated with the infantry on Snakeshead, it might have achieved some success. But the Camerons had not been consulted. The interest of the commanders, at that stage, lay elsewhere. Perhaps REVENGE should have been cancelled as was the assault of the Gurkhas from Hangman's Hill. But for a few hours the German radio crackled with a degree of excitement which almost amounted to panic.

The failures of the 19th brought the commanders a step closer to a decision to abandon the battle. Despite the change of emphasis which had emerged from Harding's appreciation in February, Fifth Army had retained the exploitation phase of DICKENS. Therefore, Freyberg had been inhibited from employing all the divisional infantry in the town. The opinion that he should do so was too strong to ignore after the 19th. It was also becoming clear that if the town could not be taken even then, the battle ought to be abandoned. In that event, there would remain the problem of tidying up the battlefield. For many of the positions which had been reached were exposed and could not be held. Hangman's Hill, Points 202 and 165 would be indefensible; the station and even the Castle would be expensive to hold, unless the German salient between the forks of Route 6 were eliminated.

Freyberg had to admit that he had either to go forward or back to his starting point. The latter was unthinkable. But even if he continued the battle, the salient he would have seized might be inadequate as a springboard for DIADEM.

It was suspected that the German salient was being continuously reinforced through tunnels which led from the Monastery and from the vicinity of the Roman Theatre to the Castle and to the Hotel des Roses. However, there was no good evidence that these tunnels existed and none at all that they were being used. It was certain, however, that the gully from Points 516 and 445 was being used to bring men and supplies into the town, and that Route 6 had not been closed either. The aim of the operations in the final stages of the battle was to seal off these routes and then to use high explosives to batter the Germans in the salient into submission.

The Castle was the key point in the infiltration route down the gully from the Monastery. But the 5th Indian Brigade declared that the Castle could not be held indefinitely if it continued to be surrounded by German posts on the steep slopes below it, from which it had been attacked several times. These posts received reinforcements down the gully and the ultimate remedy lay in occupying Points 165, 236 and the end of the Point 445 ridge. The only alternative was to evacuate the Castle. But the Germans indicated how important they considered the Castle to be by their repeated and costly attempts to take it. For if they occupied it they could make the New Zealand positions in the town untenable.

The correct conclusion seemed to be that the New Zealanders ought to clear the hillside below the Castle and that the Indians ought to take the points which controlled the gully between the Castle and the Monastery.

This might once have been within the capacity of 5th Indian Brigade. But the accomplishment of the Gurkhas in reaching and retaining Hangman's Hill had extended the Indians in another direction and now they were too weak to embark on new attacks. Up on the mountain behind the Monastery, 7th Brigade had been suffering casualties steadily and a single company was all that the 2nd/7th Gurkhas could provide for an assault on Point 445. Considering how often that ridge had withstood heavy assaults, it was unlikely to be sufficient, and it proved not to be. The

11th Brigade had already been used up to provide reinforcements for the others; 5th Brigade, spreadeagled across the hill from the Castle to Point 435, was a spent force. The solution adopted was to bring the Royal West Kents from 78th Division into the Castle and give them the task of attacking up the hill. The Essex was relieved.

Down in the town the 23rd Battalion was committed below the Castle where the 25th had been struggling for so long, and a day later the 21st was assigned the task of cutting the southern arm of Route 6 near the Hotel des Roses; with 24th Battalion it was ordered to join up with the isolated posts on the hill. The 26th Battalion, now at less than company strength, was first reinforced and later relieved at the station by the Buffs of 78th Division, in order to reduce the divisional frontage.

The fighting which occurred in the next two days confirmed the defensive strength of both sides. The Royal West Kents' attack from the Castle captured the yellow house at Point 165. But a soldier digging-in struck a mine which set off others in sympathetic detonation. Before another attack could be organised from the Castle, an assault by a company of 1st Parachute Regiment attempted to blow down the wall on the north side. Thirty-five prisoners remained behind when the Germans were forced to withdraw, and they probably suffered as many killed and wounded. The New Zealand attack along the slopes of Castle Hill had meagre success and 21st Battalion's effort made a barely perceptible advance towards the Hotel des Roses. The most significant development was the systematic destruction of German posts by very heavy and accurate tank fire. Not only were defenders seen evacuating buildings but the casualty figures for the Parachute Division rose remarkably after 20th March.

By evening on the 23rd the possibilities of the offensive had been exhausted. Freyberg and Clark considered using a brigade of 78th Division to attack over the Gari towards Route 6 between the Roman Theatre and the Hotel des Roses. But the approaches had been mined and wired, and the Gari was an obstacle to tanks, fast flowing and five feet deep. The time was past when surprise could be obtained by that move and they did not recommend it. They had also thought of using 78th Division in the Snakeshead area. But it would take too long to move the division and it would probably fail as 7th Brigade had failed. Alexander came forward to see the ground and hear the arguments in the afternoon. That evening he phoned Freyberg that, except for tidying up his position, his corps should stand firm where it then stood while arrangements were being made for XIII Corps of Eighth Army to take over the front.

That night three volunteer officers set off from the Castle to take withdrawal orders to the men on Hangman's Hill. Each had a carrier pigeon to bring back the message that the orders had been delivered. Two of them slipped through. The withdrawal was to be ordered on the 24th by radio codeword, 'Very Light' or bursts from Bofors guns. The New Zealanders on the hill below received the orders to withdraw through Major Reynolds, commanding C Company, 24th Battalion at Point 146, when he visited the Gurkhas at Hangman's Hill.

The seventh airdrop, a particularly successful one, was made on 24th March. But most of the goodies, including eight gallons of rum dropped on the New Zealanders, had to be left behind. Usually only about fifty per cent of the loads fell within reach and there was no guarantee that the most precious items could be retrieved. The Germans caused confusion by firing smoke on to Monte Trocchio of the same colours which marked the dropping zone at Cassino. But the only serious lack during the battle had been radio batteries for the

A good view of Hangmans Hill

Gurkhas, most of which floated wide. Ammunition was never short and there was plenty of water from local wells, although after the Gurkhas found a dead mule in theirs they had to rely on air supply.

Remarkably, the evacuation was achieved on the night of 24th March without a casualty. Noisy 'stoncs' (or standing linear concentrations) were laid down on the flanks of the withdrawal and the RWK entertained the enemy at Point 165 while 312 men from Hangman's Hill, Points 202 and 146, found their way back through the bottleneck at the Castle.

Not only did the parachutists not discover until the 21st that Hangman's Hill had been held by Gurkhas, but even on the 26th they were still reporting how desperately the place was being defended. And when they 'captured' it at last on the 27th, and 'mopped up' on the days following they took 'eleven prisoners and killed 165'. No doubt this fantasy was to support Heidrich's demand that everyone in his division should be promoted, without exception, and that they should wear a special sleeve badge to indicate that they had fought at Cassino. He himself received his Swords and Laurel Wreath to add to the Knight's Cross he had won in Crete in 1941. Wentzell decided to produce a history of the '2nd battle' with a 'record of the enemy divisions mauled etc.' It would 'read very nicely and, after all, the Führer wanted a success.'

A success it had certainly been and no other troops but Heidrich's could have achieved it. Only while the battle was being kept going by bogus battle reports after the 23rd did Heidrich allow the casualty figures to slip out. Then it was learned that half of 2nd/3rd Parachute had disappeared in the bombing and that the four skeleton battalions in the town then had only the strength of about two platoons each. The reserve, a battalion of 1st Parachute Regiment, was too weak to recapture Hangman's Hill. Most of 4th Parachute Regiment had had to be relieved north of the Monastery so that the division could be concentrated for the street fighting in Cassino and the defence of the hill above the town.

Senger fully expected the Allies to continue the battle after a short pause. In that event, he believed that Heidrich might hold the town for another week, after that he might hold for a short period the switch line which ran down the southern spur of Monastery Hill and through the Baron's Palace. But as 15th Panzer Grenadiers were so heavily involved behind the Monastery and in the southern outskirts of the town, and their Rapido line, south of Cassino, was stretched to breaking point, he intended to withdraw rather than to allow 90th Panzer Grenadiers to be sucked in to plug holes again.

But Alexander did not intend to resume the struggle until he had regrouped his divisions and the weather had improved. In the meantime, except for the isolated posts which had been evacuated on the 24th, not an inch of ground which DICKENS had won was to be surrendered. The positions on a line from the Castle, through the town to the area in front of the Botanical Gardens, and down to the station and the hillock, were wired and mined to prevent infiltrators. Until the front was consolidated, the tanks in the town stayed in position to continue the attrition of the enemy. The battalions in the town were then thinned out, but the New Zealand division stayed on, even though it came under the command of XIII Corps. The 4th Indian Division was relieved on the night of 26th March by 78th Division.

It was the aggressive shooting of the tanks and artillery on the days following the 23rd that deceived Heidrich into thinking that the battle was going to continue. Indeed, he was still losing men at much the same rate as before.

1939
1944
1939
1944
1944

Dickens in retrospect

The bridgehead won by the New Zealanders was not used for DIADEM. The conquest of the rest of the town was never completed and even the capture of the Monastery and the Colle Sant' Angelo by the Poles in May was not decisive. The most important operations in May were fought by the French and the Americans who broke out of the old X Corps bridgehead, and by XIII Corps which crossed the Rapido at Sant' Angelo where 36th Division had suffered in January. The positions at Cassino railway station and in the town only provided the firm flank for these operations. In this light it may appear that the blood spilt in the later battles for Cassino was wasted.

Successes and failure in the Italian campaign have to be judged by the arid statistics of casualties rather than by territory gained. The damage inflicted on 1st Parachute Division made DICKENS a successful battle of attrition. Only if it is assumed that Alexander, Freyberg and perhaps even Clark regarded it in this light, can the manner of its conduct be adequately explained.

DICKENS – a successful battle of attrition, or a waste of lives?

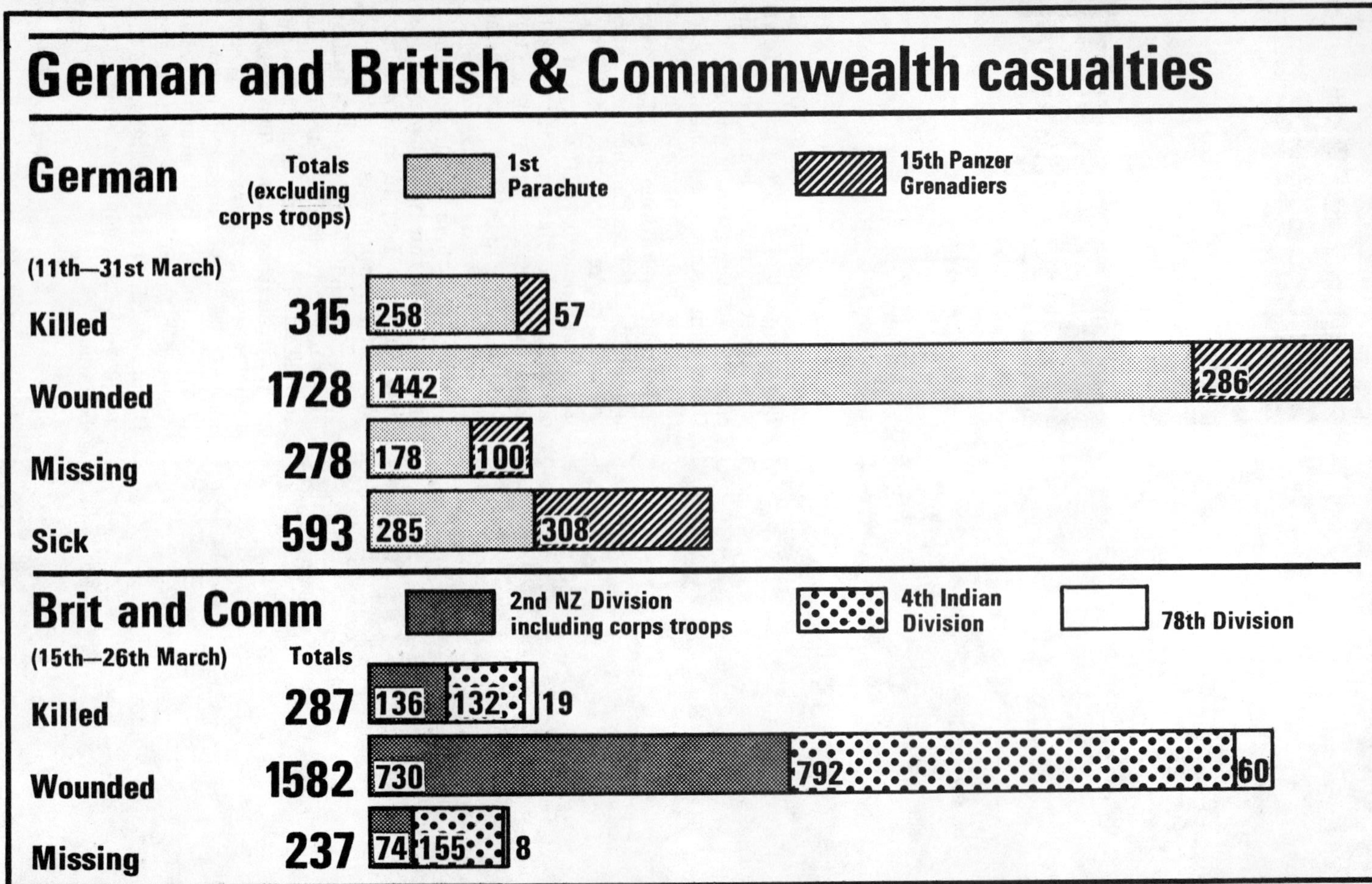

German and British & Commonwealth casualties
German
Totals (excluding corps troops)
1st Parachute
15th Panzer Grenadiers
(11th—31st March)
Killed
315
258
57
Wounded
1728
1442
286
Missing
278
178
100
Sick
593
285
308
Brit and Comm
2nd NZ Division including corps troops
4th Indian Division
78th Division
(15th—26th March)
Totals
Killed
287
136
132
19
Wounded
1582
730
792
60
Missing
237
74
155
8

The Allied commanders in Italy would not allow their men to think that they were being committed to battle simply to exchange their lives for German lives to serve a strategic purpose. Yet they could not close their eyes to the enervating implications of the explicit purpose of the campaign. This purpose was to destroy German divisions and to compel them to be replaced from outside the Italian peninsula. The acquisition of territory was only to be a means to this end.

The moral burden which this strategy laid on Alexander's shoulders was heavy. He made continual efforts to inspire his armies with a sense of purpose by giving them hope that their battles might lead to decisive victories. This simple fact has sometimes been overlaid in the effort to answer sophisticated questions about the wisdom of the campaign strategy.

During the period when SHINGLE dominated the thinking of the commanders the explicit, if intolerable, single aim of the campaign was diffused by the more exciting one of capturing Rome. In this political cause, Fifth Army suffered disproportionately in fighting for terrain in order to link up with VI Corps. Yet VI Corps, while failing to create the mobile conditions in which the German Tenth Army might have been destroyed, did contribute to the original strategic aim by forcing the Fourteenth Army to attack it. It was the only occasion on which the Germans attempted a counteroffensive and it was disastrous for them. Lucas, who was nothing if not realistic, could not understand why his superiors would not admit that he had won a great defensive battle by 19th February. But such thinking might have been politically dangerous. And there were those who, wanting to have their cake and eat it, said that the battle had been won despite Lucas' generalship. Others, equally greedy, condemned him for having fought a defensive battle at all.

At the end of February, and before the Fourteenth Army had briefly resumed its offensive on 28th February and 1st March, at a cost of another 3,000 casualties, Alexander and Harding began to restore normality to the conduct of the campaign by their new plan to prepare for a spring offensive.

Why, then, was DICKENS fought at all in mid-March?

It is clear that only the SHINGLE imperative could have induced Fifth Army to waste its strength, in the depth of winter, against the strongest position in Italy, where its material superiority was largely ineffective. DICKENS was planned after the main German offensive at Anzio had ended on 19th February but when its resumption was expected. At that stage, it was still intended that Fifth Army should break through to reach VI Corps. And the removal of General Lucas on the 22nd indicated that VI Corps was still considered to be in mortal danger.

Yet by the time that DICKENS had actually started on 15th March, after a delay of two weeks, the beachhead was safe and Alexander's new plan was beginning to take effect. Consequently the function of DICKENS in Allied strategy had changed. Now, it was primarily designed to carve out a bridgehead for DIADEM and its exploitation phase was only secondary.

Why was this change not reflected in a recasting of the plan or in the conduct of the battle?

Although Alexander's plan for future operations was not finally accepted until the end of March by the Allied Chiefs of Staff, preparatory planning in Italy was under way by the 15th. In Harding's view, the only purpose of operations before DIADEM was to set up Tenth Army for the 'kill' in the spring. The ideal situation would be that two bridgeheads over the Rapido-Garigliano existed by then. From these, lightning thrusts might envelop the Germans before they could escape to the Führer-Senger Line, which they had prepared between the Gustav and Rome. In this

A Rabbi conducts a service for the Polish Jews who died in the final battle for Montecassino

British and American war dead. The battle of attrition (à la First World War) is over

Standing in front of a Sherman tank, New Zealanders guard German prisoners

view, DICKENS was designed to provide the second of these bridgeheads over the Rapido.

The danger to the DIADEM plan was that if DICKENS weakened XIV Corp's positions to the extent that Senger considered that they would be untenable in the spring, he might order a premature retirement to the Führer-Senger Line. Consequently, an exploiting force had to be ready during the battle to prevent an orderly withdrawal. This force might bounce hastily occupied defences but it was not intended that it should join up with VI Corps or that it could fight a battle of annihilation such as was intended in the spring. At least, that was Alexander's conception. He visualized that the purpose of the operation was simply to seize a bridgehead and not to effect a junction with VI Corps in the Alban Hills. On the other hand, Clark's intentions were more ambitious. He understood that the principal purpose of DICKENS, as of AVENGER earlier, was to enable American and New Zealand armoured forces to advance up the Liri valley and to rescue the Anzio divisions. DICKENS was a continuation of the series of attempts to break through the Gustav Line.

The weakness in Alexander's concept was that Cassino town without the Monastery provided an inadequate bridgehead for DIADEM. Yet, if the Monastery positions were included, the Germans would have been so weakened that they would probably have withdrawn to a temporary switchline and then to their defences in the Führer-Senger Line. Freyberg knew that another direct assault on the Monastery would be prohibitively expensive. He believed that he could best loosen the Germans' hold on the Monastery if he broke out through the town and precipitated a general withdrawal by outflanking it. But this was not Alexander's intention at all. Yet it was difficult to envisage any better result of another battle at Cassino. The seizure of the town without the Monastery was obviously tactically unrewarding.

Freyberg was not in sympathy with Clark's view either. Because of the unsuitability of the ground for exploitation, he had been sceptical

about the value of AVENGER. The cheeseparing manner in which the New Zealanders fought that battle is an indication of it. Before the battle started he told Clark that when his division had suffered 1,000 casualties he would insist on terminating the operation. By the time DICKENS started he had already lost 500 men. The purpose of the new operation was different from AVENGER which had been simply to relieve VI Corps. DICKENS purported to be a preparation for DIADEM. It was certainly not intended to precipitate a general German withdrawal. Yet, as he thought that the scope of DICKENS could not be limited in the fashion that Alexander envisaged, Freyberg did not intend to fight a bloody battle with the only result that the Germans withdrew to a new defence line. Only a cheap break-in and a successful exploitation phase with plenty of prisoners would make New Zealand casualties in the battle supportable. Otherwise the battle appeared to be ill-conceived and he was determined to fight it on the cheap with the purpose of inflicting more casualties than he received.

Freyberg's reasoning led him to demand the bombing of the town to save casualties and to the relegation of the fight for Montecassino to second place. It also made him reluctant to commit 5th Brigade, the exploiting formation, to the fighting in the town even though its presence earlier might have been decisive. He was sceptical of the use of Cassino as a bridgehead and suspected that another battle was being fought there because there was nowhere else to go and because his troops were the only ones available. DICKENS appeared to him to be simply another Fifth Army operation in the old pattern, designed to hold Germans on the main front.

The conduct of the battle by Freyberg's subordinates reflects his attitude to it. But in some important respects they failed to apply his principles correctly. While Kippenberger still commanded the division, it was axiomatic that the success of DICKENS depended on a speedy and weighty assault after the bombing. One of the principles of street fighting is the simultaneous envelopment of the defence in depth which is achieved by continuous infiltration. But on the 15th, instead of attacking down all three roads leading to the town from the north, 6th Brigade used only Caruso Road. A and B Companies of 25th Battalion which entered on that route, did all the fighting in the town on 15th March. They can have had no decisive numerical advantage over their enemy. Even when Route 6 was cleared, fresh infantry did not enter by it, although it could have been used on the first night to support the tired and disorganised 25th Battalion and to enable an attack to be mounted between the station and the Hotel des Roses on the 16th.

It appears that 6th Brigade expected a walk-over and did not prepare for opposition by following Kippenberger's original plan. When it met resistance it was always a step behind with remedies. As the official historian wrote, part of the trouble was that battalion headquarters did not move

into the town and neither the commanding officers nor the brigadier were in touch with conditions there. In addition, the New Zealanders were not experienced street fighters, whereas 1st Parachute Division had been recently trained in the art at Ortona. Some techniques, appropriate to fighting in the open, were inapplicable in a built-up area. Tanks could not accompany the battalions on the first day, communications broke down and direct artillery support could not be utilised. Predicted fire tasks on the southern arm of Route 6 were not heavy or continuous enough to disrupt the flow of supplies and reinforcements into the town. These technical shortcomings are reasons for the inconclusive results of the battle.

The general criticism that the follow-up battalions were tardily committed and were not well positioned to jump into battle may be levelled at 5th Indian Brigade as well. But a contribution to the mishap to the Rajputana Rifles on the 15th and the late arrival of the Essex at the Castle was the congestion caused on Caruso Road by two brigades. This is another reason why 6th Brigade should have been fed into the battle by several routes as was originally planned.

In the final analysis, it is a mistake to assume that had some other course been followed DICKENS would have been more successful. Given the conflicting aims of the battle and the assumption about New Zealand casualties, it is doubtful if the purpose of the battle could have been attained even if 6th Brigade had not loaded the dice against itself. But had Kippenberger's original plan been followed, New Zealand casualties might have been lower. However, the same might have been true of the Germans. Yet the purpose of the Italian campaign was well served by DICKENS and it is a mistake to regard it as a defeat for the New Zealand Corps like AVENGER.

Mixed depression and fear on the faces of British prisoners

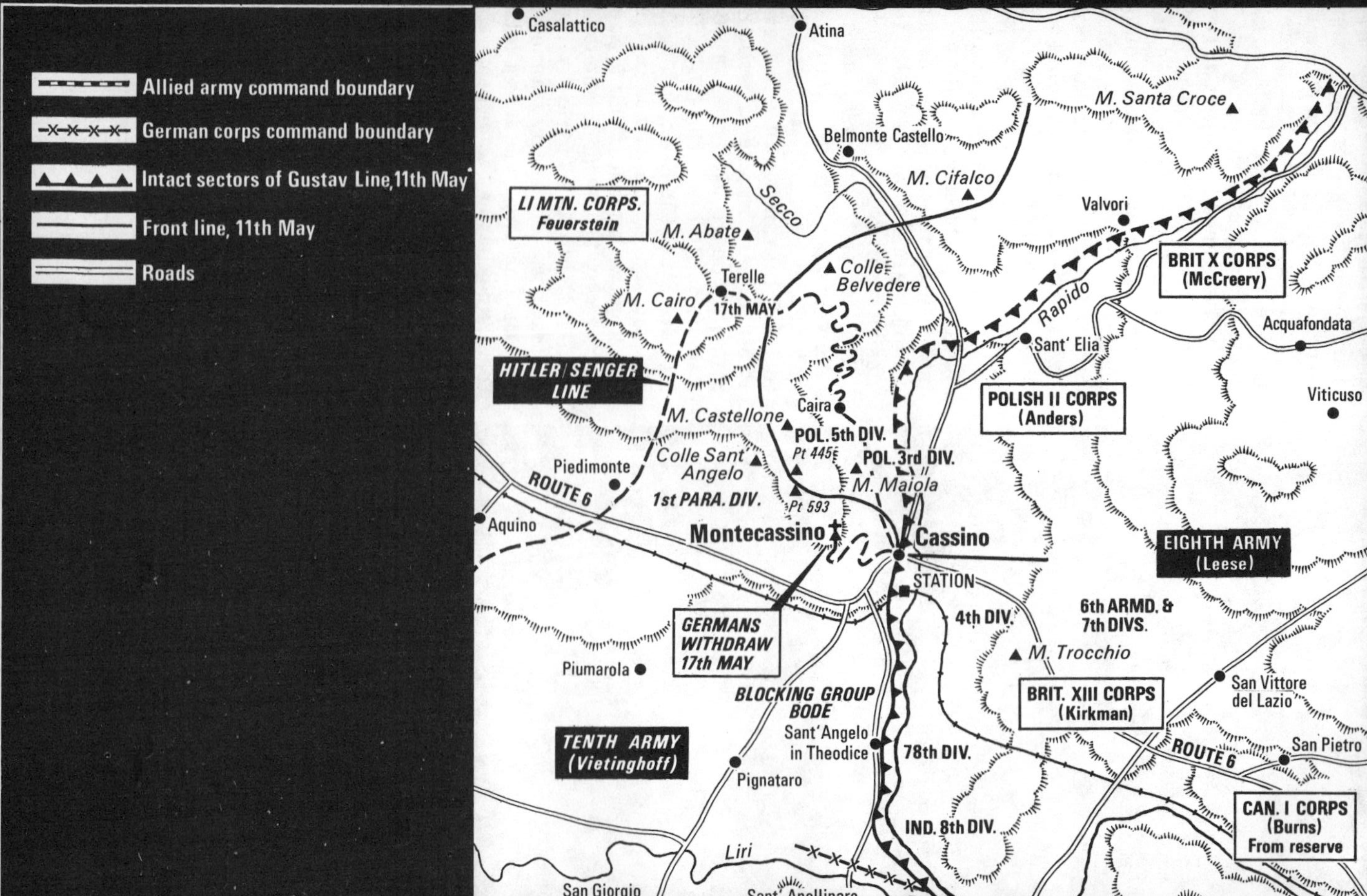

Allied army command boundary
German corps command boundary
Intact sectors of Gustav Line, 11th May
Front line, 11th May
Roads
Casalattico
Atina
M. Santa Croce
Belmonte Castello
M. Cifalco
Valvori
LI MTN. CORPS. Feuerstein
Secco
M. Abate
BRIT X CORPS (McCreery)
Terelle
Colle Belvedere
M. Cairo
17th MAY
Rapido
Acquafondata
Sant' Elia
HITLER/SENGER LINE
POLISH II CORPS (Anders)
Viticuso
Caira
M. Castellone
POL. 5th DIV.
Pt 445
POL. 3rd DIV.
Colle Sant' Angelo
Piedimonte
M. Maiola
ROUTE 6
1st PARA. DIV.
Pt 593
Aquino
Montecassino
Cassino
EIGHTH ARMY (Leese)
STATION
6th ARMD. & 7th DIVS.
4th DIV.
GERMANS WITHDRAW 17th MAY
M. Trocchio
Piumarola
San Vittore del Lazio
BLOCKING GROUP BODE
BRIT. XIII CORPS (Kirkman)
Sant'Angelo in Theodice
TENTH ARMY (Vietinghoff)
78th DIV.
ROUTE 6
San Pietro
Pignataro
CAN. I CORPS (Burns) From reserve
IND. 8th DIV.
Liri
San Giorgio
Sant' Apollinare

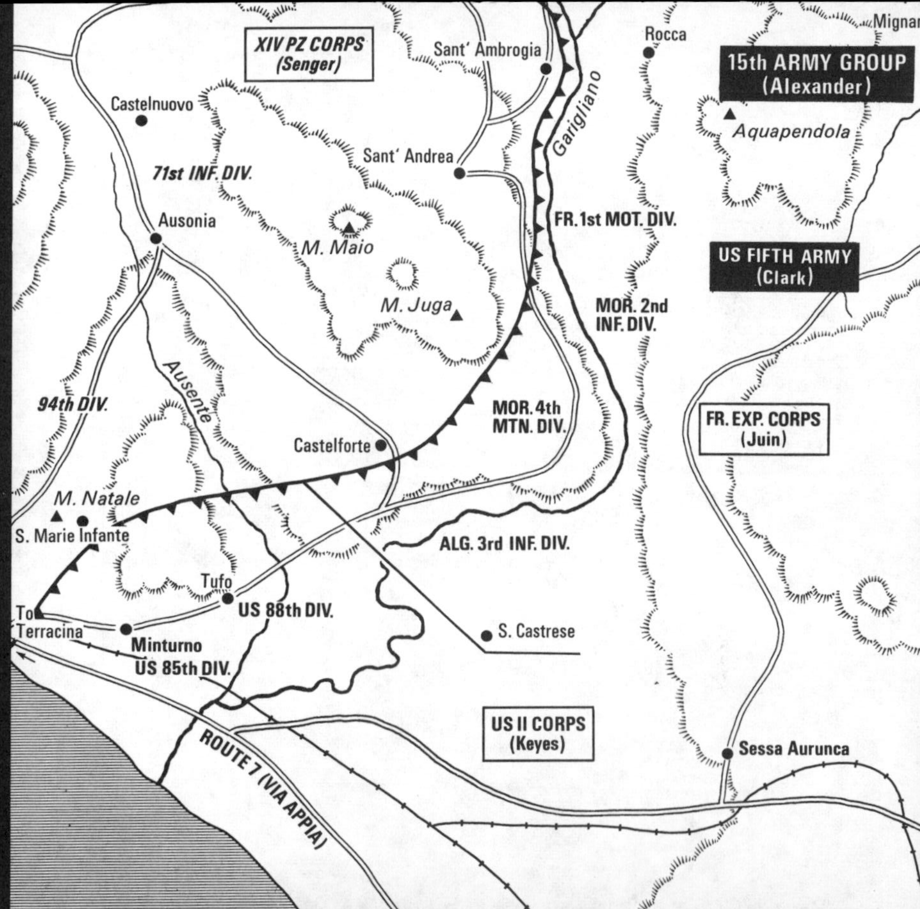

The situation before Operation Diadem

0 Miles 6

0 Kilometres 9

The bitter end

The final battle for Cassino did not play a decisive part in DIADEM although in the bitter struggle for the massif and its supporting positions the parachutists and mountain troops inflicted almost 4,000 casualties on 2nd Polish Corps. Yet the opportunity to make this sacrifice was eagerly sought by the men of an army in exile whose homeland was suffering under German occupation, and who were, in most cases, fated never to see it again.

The reorganisation of Fifteenth Army Group had brought the Poles across the mountains to relieve 78th Division north of the Monastery. The 4th British and 8th Indian Division were preparing to assault across the Rapido at Sant' Angelo, with 78th Division and 6th Armoured Division behind them. This force was to provide the left arm of pincers which would meet the Polish Corps on Route 6 at Piedimonte. The Canadian Corps with the 1st Infantry Division and the 5th Armoured Division were available for the pursuit up the Liri valley.

Further south, the French, now organised in two corps, were to make

12th May. Polish troops move up for the third (this time successful) attempt

General Sir Oliver Leese

General Anders, Polish II Corps

a surprise penetration of the mountains in order to separate the XIV Panzer Corps from its neighbour to the north, LI Mountain Corps, and reach the Senger Line before it could be occupied. The French were to join the Canadians in the Liri valley. On their left, two new American divisions, the 85th and 88th, supported if necessary by the 36th, were to advance astride Route 7.

It was assumed that the vital break would be made by Eighth Army in the Liri valley. The operations of the French and the Americans on less favourable terrain were to threaten the flank of the Germans as they retired up Route 6. Juin's two original divisions had fought with magnificent *élan* for Belvedere and had made possible 34th Division's penetration of the Cassino massif in February. Now he had two new divisions and a number of independent battalions. Not only did Juin's men have a fighting edge which the Poles, their old allies and friends, shared with them – but they were professional soldiers who could not quite conceal that they were sceptical about the ponderous methods of the Anglo-Saxons on their flanks.

In the battle, the French surprised their friends as well as their enemy by maintaining their momentum through the most difficult country with efficiency and determination. The rôle and fortunes of the Polish Corps in the sorry Cassino battlefield were less happy.

The Poles were to drive the parachutists from the Cassino massif. By occupying it they would make the German positions in the valley facing XIII Corps untenable. After the two corps met on Route 6, the Poles would advance through the foothills parallel to the road with XIII Corps on its left.

The German Tenth Army had also reorganised after DICKENS. The mobile divisions had been withdrawn from the line as far as possible and the centre of gravity of the army had been shifted south to match the similar movement in Fifteenth Army Group. The boundary between XIV Panzer Corps and LI Mountain Corps was the Liri. XIV Corps therefore faced the French and the Americans of Fifth Army and LI Corps of Eighth Army.

The 15th Panzer Grenadiers were to have been relieved by 44th Division when 5th Mountain had pinched them out by extending its front to meet Heidrich's Parachute Division north of Cassino. However, the moves of these divisions had not been completed by the time DIADEM started. The 104th Panzer Grenadier Regiment had reached 15th Division's new area on the coast near Terracina, but the other regiment, the 115th, had been split up to plug holes in the line during the winter battles and remained in the Cassino area. Two of 44th Division's regiments were still north of Cassino so that the old front of 15th Panzer Grenadiers was temporarily held by Blocking Group Bode containing parts of several divisions.

The Cassino defences were still held by Heidrich's men but they had been thinned out since DICKENS. The 100th Mountain Regiment held Castellone and the Colle Sant' Angelo and the parachutists were on the features round the Monastery, in the town, and in the reserve positions from Villa Santa Lucia along the reverse slopes towards the Monastery. It was no longer axiomatic that Cassino must be held. The question now was simply; for how long? The answer depended on how successfully the defence of the Liri valley below was conducted. The parachutists would try to hold until Bode's group disengaged and withdrew to the Führer Line.

As in previous battles, German Intelligence gave the commanders no help in determining Allied intentions. The location of the French and their strength was a complete mystery. The Poles were believed to be between Terelle and the Via Casilina but their strength was unknown. Kesselring's fear of landings in his rear had been catered to by an Allied cover plan which depicted divisions in the Salerno area rehearsing for one. Kesselring had therefore located his mobile divisions near the coast and only part of one of them, the 104th/15th Panzer Grenadiers, was south of Anzio. The Allied build-up between Cassino and the sea could not be hidden from him, but he was so misled about the timing of the attack and its intention that several of his senior commanders were on leave when the battle started in the early morning of 12th May.

II Polish Corps consisted of the Carpathian and Kresowa Divisions and the 2nd Armoured Brigade. But the infantry divisions had only two brigades and only two squadrons of tanks from the armoured brigade could be deployed in the forward area because of the difficulty of the terrain.

Because of the need to conceal their strength from the enemy, the Poles had been unable to patrol and the proximity of the German forward positions made it difficult to learn much about the ground behind them. Except for the weather, conditions were much the same as they had been in February. The steady drain of casualties from the sangars, the stench of dead bodies and the lack of hot food were still part of daily life. General Anders' tactical problem, too, was the same as his predecessors' except that he had more men and the Germans would not on this occasion be able to reinforce Cassino from other parts of the front. Therefore, success seemed to be assured – but at what price?

Anders decided to use the method which was first attempted by 34th Division (but with only weak forces) and was later advocated by General Tuker but never put to the test. He would advance along the Monte Castellone feature to the pass at the head of the re-entrant between Albaneta and Villa Sant' Angelo position from the north. Simultaneously he would attack Point 593 and Albaneta and advance down the ridge by way of Points

569 and 476 to take the Monastery. The Kresowa Division was to take the Colle Sant' Angelo and the Carpathian the other objectives.

The keys to success were to engage as many of the mutually supporting German posts as simultaneously as possible, and to rush reinforcements forward in order to catch the counter-attacking forces before they could climb back on to the objectives. This appeared to be the theoretical lesson of the past. But in practice it was difficult to attack objectives at different altitudes and on different features, many of them small and with narrow approaches, on a broad enough front. And beyond the limited vision of the men in their sangars, there was dead ground in which could lurk unseen and unpleasant surprises. In this respect, the Poles were no better placed than 7th Indian Brigade had been in February.

Knowledge of what lay in the dead ground at the south end of Monte Castellone ridge was particularly important. Air photographs and maps were not a sufficient guide alone. The expression Phantom Ridge, which appears in many accounts of the Cassino battles, illustrates the contemporary misapprehension that a defensible ridge lay between the end of Monte Castellone and the Colle Sant' Angelo. In fact the Castellone ridge broadens out and becomes a forward slope in full view of Albaneta, Point 593 and the whole length of the Colle Sant' Angelo.

It was not until they had failed at the first attempt that the Kresowa Division discovered that they must avoid 'Phantom Ridge' on their way to attack the Colle Sant' Angelo and must keep as close to the pass on the right as possible. They also learned that the attack must keep moving, as Tuker had grasped, in order to reduce the effect of flanking fire from the Old Quarry and the Passo Corno on the right and Albaneta and Points 505 and 575 on the left and ahead. There were no suitable intermediate positions between Point 706 and the final objective.

An unpleasant surprise in store for the Carpathian Division was the minefield which had been laid between Albaneta and the small pass at the head of Death Valley after REVENGE in March. The centre of the Polish attack was therefore held and the action beyond Phantom Ridge on the right paralysed. A series of German counterattacks were able to be mounted against the Carpathian battalion which had taken Point 593.

The first Polish assault on the night of 11th May and during the following day failed, not only because of the minefield and ignorance of the topography, but also because it met twice as many German battalions as had been expected. A regiment of 44th Division was being relieved by the parachutists and 100th Mountain Regiment. In all, nine battalions were engaged and mauled and the relief was seriously delayed. German counter-attacks were vigorous and heavy and were well supported by artillery because the Polish counterbattery programme silenced enemy artillery for only a short time. Polish artillery had not been well handled. Not only had the steepness of the country caused technical difficulties but also radio communications had broken down in the attack against Colle Sant' Angelo, and in consequence German counter-attacks were not broken up.

Rather than order the Poles to attack again at once, General Oliver Leese waited for XIII Corps to make some progress in the valley. Meanwhile, he told them to harass their opponent, engage his artillery and improve their knowledge of his positions.

On 16th May a second attack was ordered for early the next morning. This time the corps made no mistake. The enemy had been weakened by the first attack and a battalion of 1st

Polish and British flags on the Monastery

17th May. The town: completely gutted

Parachute Regiment had been moved down into the valley. Little more than three battalions now remained, of which one was from 3rd Parachute Regiment. The rest of the regiment was in the town.

On the 17th, 5th Kresowa Division was ordered to keep away from the so-called Phantom Ridge and work round on to the Colle Sant' Angelo without pausing. Albaneta was to be engaged by tanks while the engineers lifted the minefield and the infantry prepared to assault down the re-entrant. On the left 3rd Carpathian Division would repeat its earlier attack.

A company of 16th Battalion of the Kresowa division got the operation off to a good start. A fighting patrol captured some German positions between Point 706 and the north end of the Colle Sant' Angelo and during the night the rest of the battalion infiltrated into the area. The battle started with 2nd/100th Mountain Regiment counterattacking 16th Battalion and suffering heavily from well organised defensive fire.

The 17th Battalion passed through the 16th early in the morning and got among the Colle Sant' Angelo defences before defensive fire could be brought down. Then came the inevitable counterattacks and the Germans retook Point 517. But Polish tanks had managed to climb up above the track at the pass to Albaneta and they were able to give fire support to 17th Battalion when it was attacked from

gunners and sent them forward to help the battalions on the Colle Sant' Angelo.

While this battle was continuing the engineers had gallantly lifted the mines in front of Albaneta by lying under tanks which edged forward as the work proceeded. The success of this manoeuvre enabled the tanks to bring the rear of Point 593 under fire and to shoot the 6th Battalion of the Carpathian Division into Albaneta. But fighting for the farm and abbey continued throughout the afternoon.

As soon as Albaneta was being engaged the 4th Carpathian Battalion went forward against Point 593. The opposition proved as tough to overcome as ever and the three companies of which the battalion consisted were all required to reduce it. Counterattacks were then launched and intense fire was brought down from Point 505 and 575 on the other side of the valley. With an additional company from the 5th Battalion the position was held, but no further progress could be made down the knife-edge ridge to the Monastery. Point 569 and the positions beyond it remained in German hands. At this stage Albaneta was still holding out against the 6th Battalion below in the valley.

the direction of Point 575. Although short of ammunition, 17th Battalion held on until General Rudnicki sent the 18th Battalion forward with elements of the 16th to retake Point 517. Although they were well below strength, they succeeded and dug in there for the night.

The 13th and 14th Battalions, very weak after their efforts in the previous battle, remained firm on Point 706 and the ridge between it and the Colle Sant' Angelo. But the division had no reserves and Rudnicki expected a fierce counterattack on his forward battalions which were short of ammunition and had been reduced to throwing stones at the Germans at one stage. He organised three half-battalions from drivers, orderlies and cooks, anti-aircraft and anti-tank

While the Poles struggled on the hill, the 78th and 4th Divisions had made progress on Route 6 below them and by the evening it became necessary for Heidrich to get his men out of the trap before it closed on them. But the Poles, originally two weak divisions, were now exhausted, and Anders gave orders that during the night they were to patrol vigorously from Point 593, complete the capture of Albaneta and form up on the Colle Sant' Angelo. By these means they were to prevent the Germans from disengaging. But in the morning when the Carpathian division renewed the attack, only weak German garrisons remained in the old strongpoints. Thirty men, gaunt, hungry and mostly wounded, surrendered in the Monastery. The rest had escaped down the hill to

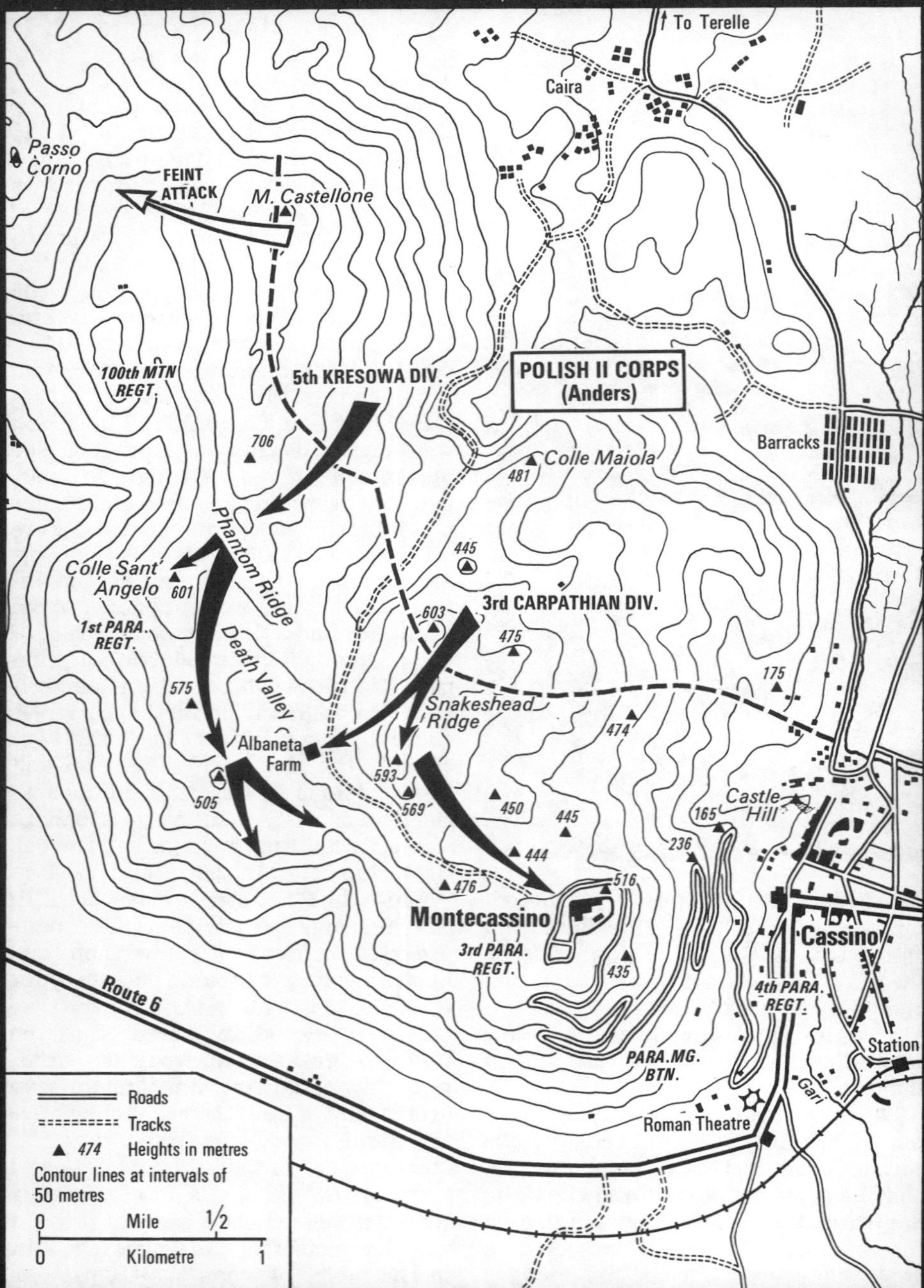

Anders' plan of attack on Montecassino

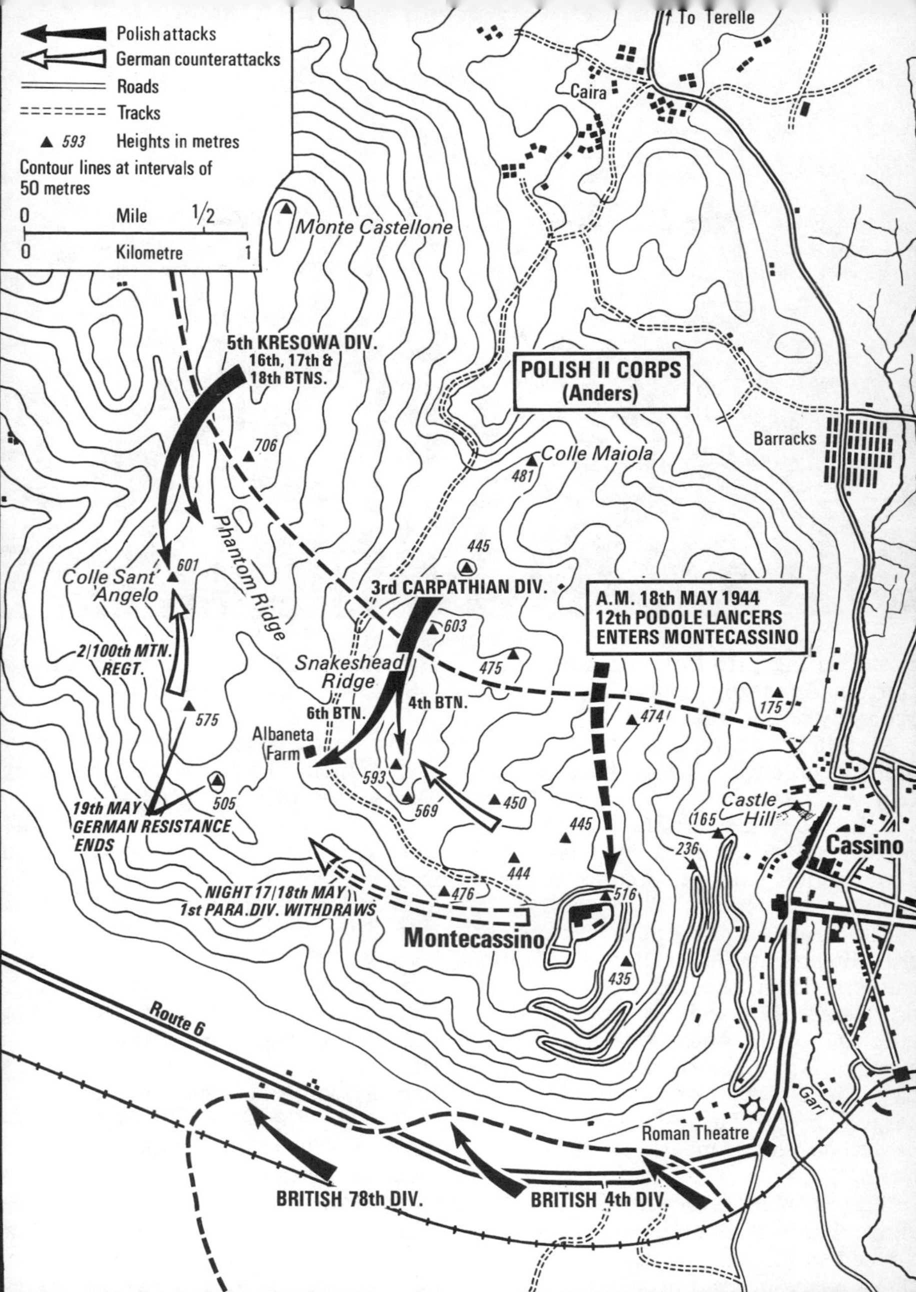

Polish II Corps enters Montecassino, but the Germans had left

17th May. The Monastery: a heap of rubble, and its art treasures ruined

avoid falling into Polish hands which they had reason to believe would probably not be kindly ones.

At 1015 hours on the 18th, the regimental colours of the 12th Podole Lancers fluttered over the ruins. Later the Polish White Eagle was proudly raised, to be followed by the Union Jack which General Anders ordered to be flown beside it.

The Kresowa division's last opponents did not surrender. It was not until the 19th that the isolated Germans on Points 575 and 505 were finally silenced. Only then was the bitter struggle for Cassino over. The next day the Polish Corps moved on to attack Piedimonte. General Anders described the scene they left behind them.

'The battlefield presented a dreary sight. There were enormous dumps of unused ammunition and here and there heaps of land mines. Corpses of Polish and German soldiers, sometimes entangled in a deathly embrace, lay everywhere, and the air was full of the stench of rotting bodies. There were overturned tanks with broken caterpillars and others standing as if ready for an attack, with their guns still pointing towards the Monastery. The slopes of the hills, particularly where the fire had been less intense, were covered with poppies in incredible number, their red flowers weirdly appropriate to the scene. All that was left of the oak grove of the so-called Valley of Death were splintered tree-stumps. Crater after crater pitted the sides of the hills, and scattered over them were fragments of uniforms and tin helmets, tommy guns, Spandaus, Schmeissers and hand-grenades.

'Of the Monastery itself there remained only an enormous heap of ruins and rubble, with here and there some broken columns. Only the western wall, over which two flags flew, was still standing. A cracked church bell lay on the ground next to an unexploded shell of the heaviest calibre, and on shattered walls and ceilings fragments of paintings and frescoes could be seen. Priceless works of art, sculpture, pictures and books lay in the dust and broken plaster.'

Bibliography

Salerno to Cassino Martin Blumenson (OCMH, Washington)
Anzio, the Gamble That Failed Martin Blumenson (Weidenfeld & Nicolson, London. Lippencott, Philadelphia)
The Official History of New Zealand in the Second World War, Volume I N C Phillips (Wellington, 1957)
The Fourth Indian Division G R Stevens (Toronto)
The Battle for Italy W G F Jackson (Batsford, London. Harper-Row, New York)
The Battle for Rome W G F Jackson (Batsford, London, Scribner, New York)
Cassino: Portrait of a Battle Fred Majdalany (Panther, London)
Monte Cassino Charles Connell (London, 1963)
Neither Hope Nor Fear F von Senger und Etterlin (London, 1963)
Soldier to the Last Day Albert Kesselring (London, 1954)
Montecassino R Bohmler (London, 1964)
The Campaign in Italy Eric Linklater (HMSO, London)